SOUTH WEST COAST PATH

Minehead to Padstow

SOUTH WEST COAST PATH

Minehead to Padstow

Roland Tarr

Photographs by Mike Williams
General editor Michael Allaby

AURUM PRESS

COUNTRYSIDE COMMISSION · ORDNANCE SURVEY

ACKNOWLEDGEMENTS

My thanks to the following organisations and people for help and advice:
Richard Brooks, Jim Webber & Tim Braund, Exmoor National Park; Dave
Edgecombe of the North Devon Heritage Coast; Tom Hynes of the Hartland
Heritage Coast; Alan Dixon of the Tarka Trail; Simon Ford of the National
Trust; Charlie David & Tim Dingle of the North Cornwall Heritage Coast;
Sarah Welton and Joan Edwards for the article on marine wildlife; and Peter
Woodward for checking historical information.

Roland Tarr was born and brought up in West Somerset and has close family
ties with Exmoor. He was Heritage Coast Officer in Dorset from 1974 to 1988.

First published 1990 by Aurum Press Ltd in association with the
Countryside Commission and the Ordnance Survey. This revised edition
first published 1996.

Ordnance Survey, Pathfinder and Travelmaster are registered trade marks
and the OS symbol, Explorer and Outdoor Leisure are trade marks of
Ordnance Survey, the national mapping agency of Great Britain.
A catalogue record for this book is available from the British Library

ISBN 1 85410 415 2

Book design by Robert Updegraff
Cover photograph: Woody Bay (by Roy Westlake)
Title page photograph: Ilfracombe from Hillsborough.

Typeset by Wyvern 21 Ltd, Bristol
Printed and bound in Italy by Printer Trento Srl

CONTENTS

Circular walks appear on pages 27, 28, 36, 56, 66, 120, 128, 159

How to use this guide

The 613-mile (987-kilometre) South West Coast Path is covered by four national trail guides. Each guide describes a section of the path between major estuaries. This book describes the path from Minehead to Padstow, 163 miles (262 kilometres).

This guide is in three parts:

• The introduction, historical background to the area and advice for walkers.

• The path itself, described in thirteen chapters, with maps opposite each route description. This part of the guide also includes information on places of interest as well as a number of related short walks, either starting from the path itself or at a car park. Key sites are numbered in the text and on the maps to make it easy to follow the route description.

• The last part includes useful information such as local transport, accommodation, organisations involved with the path, and further reading.

The maps have been prepared by the Ordnance Survey for this trail guide using 1:25000 Pathfinder®, Explorer™ and Outdoor Leisure™ maps as a base. The line of the Coast Path is shown in yellow, with the status of each section of the path – footpath or bridleway for example – shown in green underneath (see key on inside front cover). These rights of way markings also indicate the precise alignment of the path at the time of the original surveys, but in some cases the yellow line on these maps may show a route which is different from that shown by those older surveys, and in such cases walkers are recommended to follow the yellow route in this guide, which will be the route that is waymarked with the distinctive acorn symbol 🌰 used for all national trails. Any parts of the path that may be difficult to follow on the ground are clearly highlighted in the route description, and important points to watch for are marked with letters in each chapter, both in the text and on the maps. *Some maps start on a right-hand page and continue on the left-hand page – black arrows (➡) at the edge of the maps indicate the start point.* Should there have been a need to alter the route since publication of this guide for any reason, walkers are advised to follow the waymarks or signs which have been put up on site to indicate this. Since the Coast Path passes through a military exercise area at Braunton Burrows, walkers are advised to pay particular heed to any signs posted and flags flying relating to entry to the area when firing is taking place.

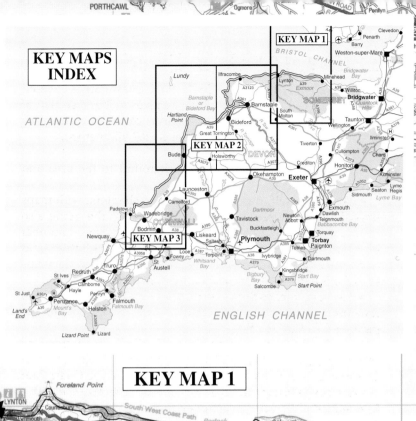

KEY MAPS INDEX

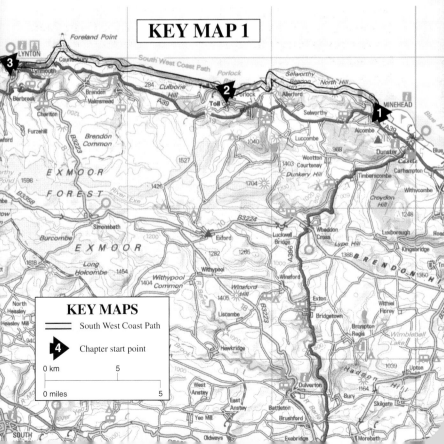

KEY MAP 1

KEY MAPS

South West Coast Path

4 Chapter start point

0 km — 5

0 miles — 5

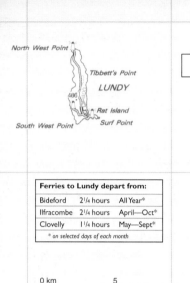

North West Point

Tibbett's Point

LUNDY

466

Rat Island

South West Point   Surf Point

KEY MAP 2

Ferries to Lundy depart from:

Bideford	2¼ hours	All Year*
Ilfracombe	2¼ hours	April—Oct*
Clovelly	1¼ hours	May—Sept*

* on selected days of each month

0 km   5

0 miles   5

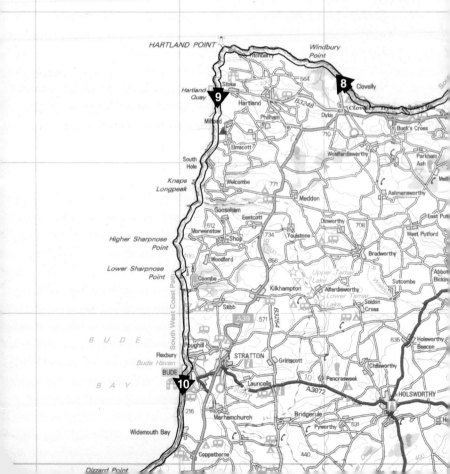

BARNSTAPLE

OR

BIDEFORD

BAY

HARTLAND POINT

Windbury
Point

Hartland
Quay

Stoke

9

Hartland

Philham

B3248

Dyke

Clovelly

8

Clovelly Dyke

Buck's Mill

Buck's Cross

Milford

Elmscott

Philham

710

Woolfardisworthy

Parkham
Ash

South
Hole

Welcombe

771

Meddon

Ashmansworthy

Mell

Knaps
Longpeak

Gooseham

Eastcott

Dinworthy

708

East Putt

Higher Sharpnose
Point

512

Morwenstow

Shop

734

Youlstone

West Putford

Woodford

656

Bradworthy

Lower Sharpnose
Point

400

Coombe

Upper Tamar
Lake

Sutcombe

Abbot
Bickin

Kilkhampton

Alfardisworthy

Lower Tamar
Lake

Soldon
Cross

BUDE

Stibb

571

B3254

A39

635

Holsworthy
Beacon

Poughill

STRATTON

Grimscott

Chilsworthy

Flexbury

Bude Haven

BUDE

10

10

Pancrasweek

A3072

HOLSWORTHY

BAY

216

Launcells

Marhamchurch

Bridgerule

Pyworthy

531

He

Widemouth Bay

Coppethorne

440

South West Coast Path

Dizzard Point

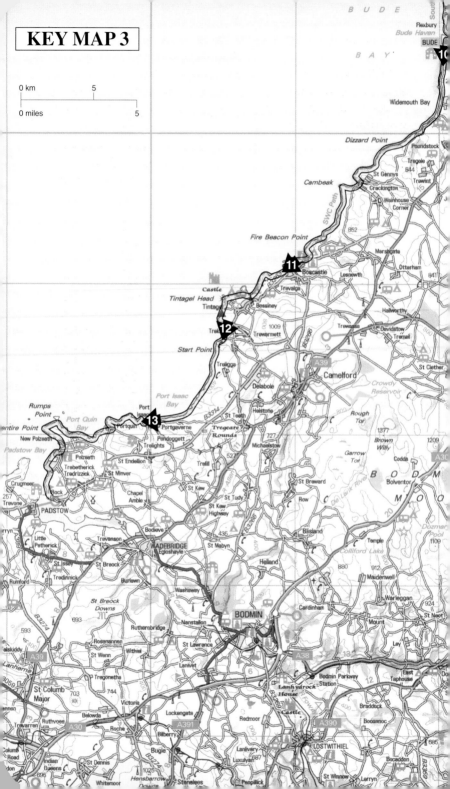

Distance checklist

This list will assist you in calculating the distances between places on the Coast Path where you may be planning to stay overnight, or in checking your progress along the way.

location	approx. distance from previous location	
	miles	km
Minehead	0	0
Bossington	6.2	10.0
Porlock Weir	2.4	3.9
Culbone	1.6	2.6
Lynmouth Harbour	10.5	16.9
Lynton	0.4	0.6
Combe Martin	12.3	19.8
Ilfracombe	5.3	8.5
Woolacombe	7.7	12.4
Saunton	8.3	13.4
Braunton	7.6	12.2
Barnstaple (Long Bridge)	5.4	8.7
Bideford	9.5	15.3
Appledore	3.1	5.0
(from Barnstaple via Instow Ferry)	(7.1)	(11.4)
Westward Ho!	4.9	7.9
The Hobby Drive	8.5	13.7
Clovelly	2.6	4.2
Hartland Point	7.2	11.6
Hartland Quay	2.6	4.2
Devon/Cornwall county boundary	5.7	9.2
Bude (canal lock)	9.3	15.0
Crackington Haven	9.4	15.1
Boscastle Harbour	7.1	11.4
Rocky Valley	2.5	4.0
Tintagel Haven	2.2	3.5
Trebarwith Strand	1.9	3.1
Portgaverne	5.7	9.2
Port Isaac	0.7	1.1
Portquin	3.3	5.3
Polzeath	5.5	8.8
Padstow–Rock (ferry)	2.8	4.5

Preface

The South West Coast Path follows the spectacular fringe of one of Britain's most popular coastal holiday areas from Minehead in Somerset, through Devon and Cornwall to Poole Harbour in Dorset. The section covered in this book, from Minehead to Padstow, skirts the edge of Exmoor before dropping down past Bideford to Hartland, Bude and Tintagel Head.

The path is notable for its spectacular cliffs and fine sandy beaches and the presence of circular walks inland make it attractive to day trippers as well as long-distance walkers.

Local Authorities work with organisations such as the National Trust to maintain the path using Countryside Commission funding. The exposed nature of the path and its popularity make this a major task in some areas. The path is waymarked with a distinctive acorn symbol which signals that you are on the right route.

I hope you will enjoy using this book during many hours of walking on this delightful stretch of England's coastline for which I have great personal affection.

Richard Simmonds
Chairman
Countryside Commission

PART ONE

INTRODUCTION

The landscape along the Coast Path

Dramatic heights and stunning views into the distance are the main feature of this part of the South West Coast Path. In the Exmoor National Park the Coast Path climbs several times to over 1,000 feet (300 metres) and the highest point on the whole of the Coast Path, the Great Hangman, is just east of Combe Martin, at 1,043 feet (318 metres). Sometimes the path runs along the steep clifftop slopes at around the 700-foot (210-metre) mark. This part of the walk is not for the nervous. On Exmoor you may see red deer, Britain's largest wild land animal, in the woods between Lynton and Minehead.

From Exmoor, views of the Gower Peninsula in South Wales and the Glamorgan Heritage Coast, with the lighthouse at Nash Point in the centre and limestone cliffs on either side, can be seen with startling detail on a clear day. Gradually going west, the landscape softens around Ilfracombe and Mortehoe, with lower cliffs but a series of tiny coves and headlands, every one with its own character, distinctive wildlife, and pleasing views. On very clear days the view from Bull Point and Baggy Point extends to the cliffs of Pembrokeshire. With Hartland Point on the extreme left, Lundy due west, and the Gower Peninsula to the north-east, a good pair of binoculars will pick up the high chimneys of the refineries at Milford Haven, with the cliffs of south Pembrokeshire becoming clearly visible not far to the east of this.

A visit to the Isle of Lundy could be included by taking a boat trip from Ilfracombe or Bideford. Just a little further south, the cliffs from Westward Ho! to the Devon border south of Hartland Point, with the path passing through the lovely village of Clovelly, must be one of the most beautiful coastal walks in England.

Once into Cornwall, the path runs south virtually all the way to Padstow, giving views of yet more dramatic cliffs. Bude has sandy beaches but south from there to Padstow the coast is wild, rocky, high – over 700 feet (210 metres) in places – and sometimes remote.

Boscastle has one of the most beautiful natural harbours and the young Thomas Hardy, architect and hopeful author, loved to walk there. Tintagel has fine cliff scenery and a dramatic castle. The tourist paraphernalia can be off-putting but, in spite of that, the verbal tradition of the existence of a King Arthur, his knights and his Round Table is an interesting and intriguing tale that bears study and is the subject of some of the major epics of European literature.

South of Tintagel, the tiny fishing villages of Portgaverne, Port Isaac and Portquin give a taste of villages that will be seen further south in Cornwall. The harbours along the route still show many signs of ancient sea-trading with places as far away as America.

The driftwood-built Parson Hawker's hut, Vicarage Cliff, Morwenstow, where he wrote some of his poetry.

The Packhorse Bridge at Allerford.

A fine way to start this walk would be to ride on the West Somerset Railway, pulled along in carriages of 1950s vintage by a grand old Great Western steam engine. If you arrive in Taunton by train (Taunton has excellent services from all parts of the country) you can catch a bus to Bishops Lydeard to start this journey.

Planning your walk

Each of the chapters describes one day's easy walking, an average of 10 to 12 miles (16 to 19 km). This allows you to spend time looking at some of the wildlife, the geology, the architecture of the small village churches, or any of the fascinating things that may catch your eye. Allow about a fortnight to savour fully all that this path has to offer.

What time of year is best? Autumn and winter are without a doubt the most dramatic times to walk. You will see the North Devon and Cornwall coasts at their wildest and most majestic, and often have the path to yourself. In the estuaries you will see many species of wintering birds. Spring is good for flowers and watching the cliff-nesting birds and, taking care to avoid public holidays, the cliffs will be relatively uncrowded, particularly on weekdays. Early summer is also a good time for the wild flowers. Midsummer and autumn can be very peaceful and often warm, but August can be overcrowded.

Equipment

This is one of the mildest parts of the United Kingdom. In winter, when the most beautiful views will be obtained, you should of course allow for the possibility of freezing weather. If you can afford it, a top-grade down jacket with a hood, which can be reduced to a minimal size when packed tightly into a purpose-made bag, can guarantee warmth whatever the conditions.

When it rains, good-quality waterproofs make an enormous difference to your enjoyment of the walking. Plastic waterproofs, which you may use for short excursions near home, can be extremely sweaty and uncomfortable when you are fighting your way from sea level to 500 feet (150 metres) during a sudden downpour or, worse still, when it decides to rain all day. Some form of breathable waterproof gear is much better. There are several makes on sale in good camping shops. It may seem an expensive purchase at first but, having bought it, you will never again worry about a rainy day.

In addition to bird and flower books, try to take a pair of miniature binoculars that you can carry in your pocket.

Some stretches could be walked in trainers during a dry period. Much better, however, would be leather walking shoes with commando-style grips, or mountain boots. These will stop you slipping on the steep slopes, making your walk easier as well as safer. Always 'run them in' for three or four days, even if it means wearing them around the house: it will save endless blisters and discomfort at the beginning of your walking holiday.

As most of the directions in this guide use 'north, south, east, west' terminology you may find a compass useful.

Camping

For camping, a 75-litre rucksack during the winter and a 50-litre rucksack during the summer is recommended. The maximum weight, including tent, sleeping bag, all spare clothing and cameras, need not exceed 28 pounds (13 kilograms). It is amazing how little you need to exist for days on end!

There are many camp sites along the way but, if it is not possible to reach one, farmers along the route are often happy to give permission to *bona fide* walkers.

St Nectan's Glen.

Youth hostels and bed and breakfast

If you are youth hostelling or staying in bed and breakfast accommodation, all you need is warm gear for cold days, waterproofs, a camera, this guide, and good bird and flower guides.

Booking is essential during school holiday periods and summer weekends (see page 164), but during the rest of the year walking can be much more relaxed and flexible if you stay each night wherever the fancy takes you.

For bed and breakfast in the villages it is best to enquire at the village shop, post office or pub. This is a long-established holiday area and you should have few problems.

Don't forget that many farmhouses lie in magnificent settings just beside the Coast Path, and that some of them do Farmhouse Bed and Breakfast. Many of the farming families will have been here for generations, and you'll experience English rural life at first hand. Ask local Tourist Information Centres for details.

Safety precautions

Sensible walkers need have little to worry about on safety grounds. However, there are a few accidents each year. None of the cliffs of this coast is stable at any time.

Rock falls often consist of many thousands of tons of rock. People who do not keep well away from the base of higher cliffs, especially when spending a large part of one day in the same place, are at particular risk.

The other cause of accidents is the inadvertent slip on steep ground or tripping over, often the result of looking at the view instead of the path. In case of serious injury, a whistle may be useful to attract attention if you are alone, as well as a first-aid kit. It is advisable to let people know where you are going, for the same reason. Swimming is generally safe on incoming tides in the coves. On exposed parts of the coast, watch the water carefully for currents and observe any warning signs.

Walking along the sandy beaches at Woolacombe, Croyde and Saunton is usually feasible and one can always escape via the dunes if the tide starts coming in. On the rockier shores with cliffs, following the shoreline between beaches can be extremely dangerous. Almost every year someone is cut off by the tide or caught by an unexpected wave somewhere on the coast of Cornwall and Devon when attempting to do this without sufficient local knowledge.

PART TWO

SOUTH WEST COAST PATH
Minehead to Padstow

1 Minehead to Porlock Weir

passing Bossington
8½ miles (13.8 km)

The official Coast Path starts from Minehead seafront halfway between the station and the harbour **1**, just north of the Red Lion Hotel, where there is a brown sign proclaiming (inaccurately!) 'Coast Path to Poole 500 miles'.

Follow the donkey track up the alley between black and white poles to the left of a thatched cottage. Turn right to rise through the pinewood. Go up the steps and turn right (westwards) to continue, and left and right briefly to keep parallel with the

Contours are given in metres
The vertical interval is 10m

coast. Carry on straight ahead above the small public garden until the Coast Path zigzags steeply up to a hairpin bend on a tarmac road. A tarmac track keeping on the level and going westwards leaves the road at this point. This is the Coast Path.

Still keeping parallel to the coast, and well above the sea, you will come to the cairn marking the Exmoor National Park boundary with its distinctive deer head and antlers. Here take the higher track rising westwards. Where it starts to descend, fork along a path which eventually emerges from the trees on to the gorse- and bracken-covered slopes of North Hill.

As the steep Burgundy Chapel **2** path joins from the right (north), the Coast Path turns briefly inland for a hundred yards and then turns right at the next junction to continue due west **A**. At the next junction after that leave the more rugged clifftop route to the seaward side (unless you intend to take this more dramatic and wild alternative, of which details are given on page 28). Keep straight on and you will come into sight of a deep, wide combe with some woodland running up the middle and smaller combes dividing from it. Go through a bridle gate to keep inland of the green grassy area ahead and stay just to the landward side of the fields for 2 miles (3 km). You will be able to see Dunkery Beacon to the south-west and Selworthy Beacon

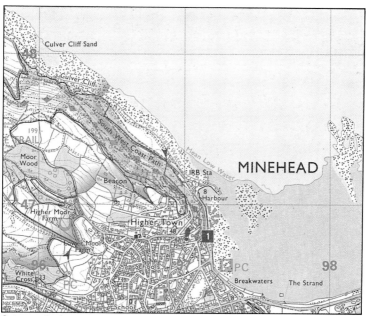

Contours are given in metres
The vertical interval is 10m

23

behind you. The farmhouses at West Myne and East Myne are now deserted, but you will see on the map their two names, pronounced in West Somerset dialect as Main. 'Mynedd' is hill in Welsh, hence the name Minehead.

When you see a Second World War underground installation **B** and a car park to the left (south) you are north of Selworthy **3**. Fork right and keep along the shoulder until the path divides, go left and down through the middle of a dry valley (Hurlstone Combe) with gorse and heather slopes to the cliff edge, and there branch left (south) to walk half a mile (1 km) to Bossing-

Contours are given in metres
The vertical interval is 10m

ton. At Bossington there are cream teas and accommodation. Just to the south-east of Bossington is Lynch, where there is a Chapel of Ease **4**, built around 1530.

The shingle ridge at Porlock has been breached due to winter storms. The official trail route is impassable; DO NOT ATTEMPT TO CROSS THE BREACH AT ANYTIME. The Exmoor National Park Authority has erected advisory notices and a temporary alternative route is signposted to Porlock Weir via Porlock. Any further amendments on the ground will be clearly signed and waymarked.

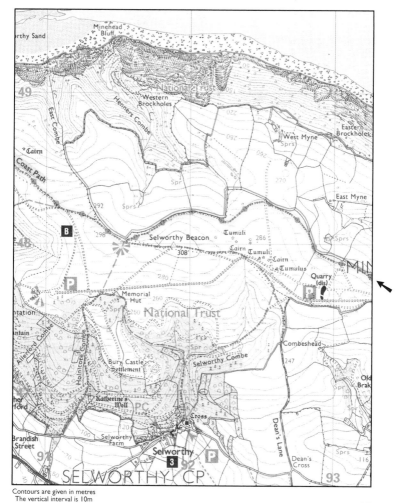

Contours are given in metres
The vertical interval is 10m

Porlock Weir – such Bristol Channel ports were busy with farm produce, coal and fish shipments until early this century.

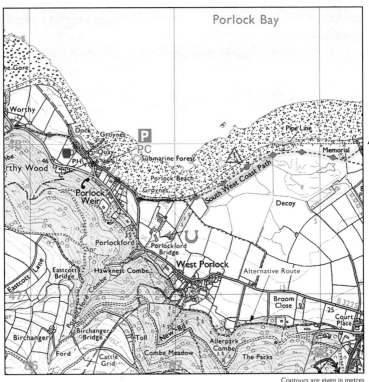

Contours are given in metres
The vertical interval is 10m

A CIRCULAR WALK FROM MINEHEAD

4 miles (6.4 km)

After exploring Minehead Harbour (see map on page 23) you can stay by the sea under Culver Cliff Wood, keeping just above the pebble beach to the western end of the lawns. Take the path up through the holm-oak and sycamore wood. This soon joins a cart road that keeps parallel to the sea at an even height, past the National Trust sign for Greenaleigh Point. Keep straight on (west) through the farmyard, following the sign to Burgundy Chapel **2**.

Shortly after passing the National Trust sign indicating that you are leaving their property at Greenaleigh Point, the path comes to a small spring above a tiny gulley and stream. Burgundy Chapel lies just below. It is late medieval and was dedicated to the Holy Trinity.

To rejoin the Coast Path, strike directly away from the sea to the south up a very steep path through the gorse. At the top you will come to a bench. Turn left to rejoin the Coast Path, and continue south and away from the sea for a few yards to a multiple junction of tracks **A**. Turn left (east) if you intend to make this into a round walk back to Minehead and right (west) if you either want a longer round walk via Hurlstone Point (see page 28) or wish to continue on the Coast Path westwards.

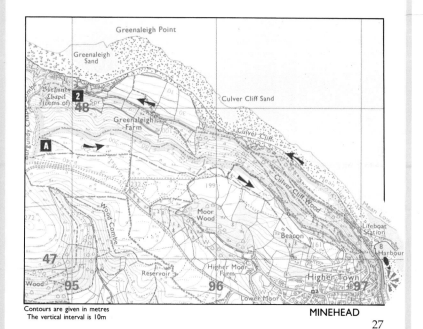

Contours are given in metres
The vertical interval is 10m

MINEHEAD

A CIRCULAR WALK OR ALTERNATIVE CLIFFTOP ROUTE TO HURLSTONE POINT

6¼ miles (10.6 km)

Park at the National Trust car park above Combeshead and go north along one of the tracks across open country until you come to the fence surrounding the green fields of East and West Myne. Turn right (east) and follow the track until you reach a grassy path leading towards the sea. You follow this to a stile giving access to the area of grassland where you fork right (north-west). Make your way gradually down the bracken- and gorse-covered combe before you. Soon you will be overlooking Grexy Combe and the junction of two streams, which you cross, rising steeply west and keeping a traditional stone wall to your left.

The path continues up the hill, gradually turning towards the sea before it turns left (west) to keep parallel to the coast, just

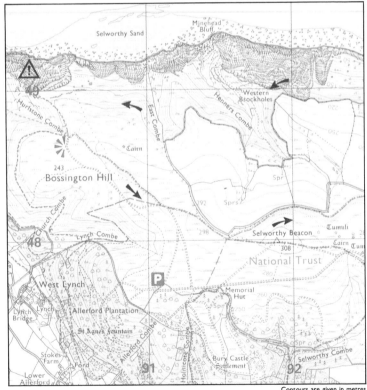

Contours are given in metres
The vertical interval is 10m

outside the stone field boundaries at the top of the extremely steep coastal slope.

One mile (1.6 km) along this route yet another deep combe opens before you. Turn inland to go round it, keeping more or less on the level before dropping briefly but steeply to cross the stream below, then keep once more parallel to the coast before crossing another small stream and returning north-westwards to the clifftop slopes. Directly across the Bristol Channel you may identify the white lighthouse at Nash Point, on the Glamorgan Heritage Coast.

Skirt round the back of East Combe, a hanging valley, keeping close to the field boundary, until you cross a stile and turn once again seaward, keeping your height or rising slightly to follow the track along the top western edge. After leaving this steep coastal combe, keep parallel to the sea and westwards to rejoin the Coast Path. Then walk back 2 miles (3 km) to the car park where you started, following the carved wooden signs.

Contours are given in metres
The vertical interval is 10m

Conserving the north coasts of Somerset, Devon and Cornwall

The Coast Path is officially looked after by the relevant local authority and the Countryside Commission reimburses a percentage of the costs. The Countryside Commission is the government-financed organisation responsible for conserving the countryside and improving access and facilities for people to enjoy it, and has played a vital role in linking all the footpaths which go together to make up the South West Coast Path.

The county wildlife trusts, the British Trust for Conservation (BTCV), and the Royal Society for the Protection of Birds (RSPB) give much help and advice. Cooperation between landowners, farmers, local authorities, the National Park Authority and heritage coast organisations, the various civic amenity and civic societies of towns and villages along the route, and many hundreds of individuals, have been a prime factor in the successful protection of this coastline.

The Coast Path mostly lies within the Exmoor National Park from Minehead to Combe Martin.

The National Park exists for the purposes of conserving and enhancing the natural beauty, wildlife and cultural heritage of Exmoor and promoting opportunities for the understanding and enjoyment of the special qualities of Exmoor by the public. The National Park Authority works with other organisations to fulfil these purposes whilst having regard to the social and economic well-being of the local population.

The North Devon, Hartland, and North Cornwall Heritage Coast and Countryside Service organisations coordinate paid staff and volunteers in a wide range of similar conservation and information work, with a strong emphasis on local involvement and consultation, practical action and protection through planning policies.

The Tarka Trail consists of 180 miles (288 km) of footpath, bridleway and rail link connecting locations in Henry Williamson's novel *Tarka the Otter*. The Trail passes through a rich variety of countryside, the saltmarsh of the Taw and Torridge estuaries, and through valleys of ancient woodland. The 23 miles (30 km) of trail between Barnstaple and Meeth follow a disused railway, re-opened in 1992 as a cycle/walkway.

The Devon and Cornwall Rail Partnership was created in 1991 as a national pilot project to encourage use of the two counties' rural railways. It is supported by both County Councils, Dartmoor National Park, Plymouth City Council, Wales and West Passenger Trains and the University of Plymouth and seeks to improve access to rural areas for leisure and recreation, improve the viability of rural transport, bring economic benefits and encourage sustainable tourism.

The National Trust was founded in 1895 as a non-profit-making voluntary association, independent of government, to acquire and protect land and buildings of national importance. In 1965 the Trust launched Enterprise Neptune the aim of which was to acquire the most beautiful stretches of coastline. Their action is complementary to that of the other organisations mentioned here, which work with all the owners and occupiers, whilst the National Trust and their Enterprise Neptune give that added protection which only ownership can ensure.

English Nature is the official organisation responsible for the conservation of the flora and fauna and geologically important sites throughout England, and for advising the government on relevant subjects. Sites of Special Scientific Interest are designated by them and strict guidelines are laid down for their protection. Many areas along this path are designated as SSSIs. English Nature also establishes and manages National Nature reserves. The next few years will see the designation of Special Areas of Conservation (SAC) – exciting because this European designation will also include marine sites here below the low water-mark.

'Countryside Stewardship' is another part of the strategy designed primarily to protect and enhance the landscape by agreements with farmers and landowners. This measure will also have benefits for wildlife. It was initially overseen by the Countryside Commission and was handed over to the Ministry of Agriculture on 1 April 1996. You will see many areas defined by on-site maps along the route.

Long Island, Trevalga, from Trewethett.

2 Porlock Weir to Lynmouth Harbour

via Culbone
12 miles (19.3 km)

At Porlock Weir go up behind the Anchor Hotel, through a gate, straight on along the side of the field behind red-tiled former stables, and over a stile. Here a path comes up from the harbour.

Go through another stile at the western end of the field and follow the landward side of a hedge to a gate. Then keep to the higher side of a triangular field to the gate at the far end and join a lane. Follow this lane straight ahead (west) until you come to the arches of the Worthy Combe Toll Lodge. Go through the right-hand archway gate and follow the estate ride.

Arched over by rhododendron, oak and pine, the path goes by whimsical arched grottoes and turreted lookouts. These were the creation of Lord Lovelace, who spent much time in Italy and was inspired by the romantic landscapes there. The path soon zigzags up through the steep slope of the woods to join a higher track west **A** (right) to Culbone with a further short diversion at **B** before continuing along an original path.

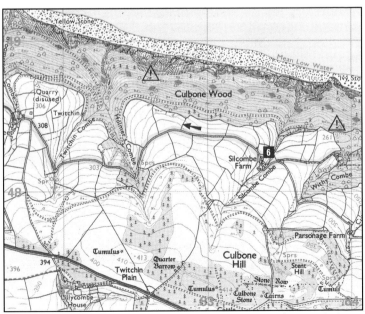

Contours are given in metres
The vertical interval is 10m

Half a mile (1 km) further on you will see Culbone Church **5** (see page 45) down below, accompanied by the sound of the small stream tumbling down to the sea. This is the smallest complete parish church in England, being only 35 feet long and 12 foot 4 inches wide in the nave.

From the church, follow the track which climbs up behind the cottages. For many years, the route through Culbone Woods has experienced severe landslips. The Exmoor National Park Authority continually monitors the slips and has engaged geological consultants who give specialist, expert advice. Where slips affect the official path, alternative routes will be signed and waymarked. Please follow these temporary routes and do not attempt to use the closed paths. After a short while you keep right and carry straight on westwards and parallel to the sea, more or less keeping to the contours for the next 2 miles (3 km) through Culbone Wood and Embelle Wood, crossing streams racing down to the sea below Silcombe, Twitchin and Broomstreet.

Alternatively, if you want to see the clifftop Exmoor farms over the next couple of miles, or need farmhouse accommodation, follow the sign left to Silcombe **6** at the junction mentioned above, and follow the round walk directions on the next page, returning to the coastal woodlands at Yenworthy. This alternative

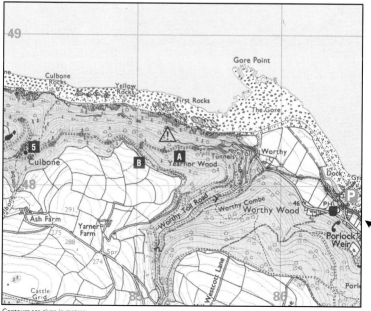

Contours are given in metres
The vertical interval is 10m

A CIRCULAR WALK FROM PORLOCK WEIR VIA CULBONE

7 miles (11.3 km)
(See maps on pages 34, 35 and 37)

Park at Porlock Weir and follow the Coast Path directions as far as Culbone Church. Keep following Coast Path to the west of Culbone but then take the upper track signed for Silcombe when you come to the first distinctive junction. This track doubles back on itself and rises steadily to follow the valley upstream from the church. Now follow the bridleway west above the deep valley of Withy Combe. Withy is the old name for willow. Soon you will briefly join the surfaced access road to Silcombe Farm (accommodation). You are now almost exactly half way between Minehead and Lynton. Continue westwards past the farm and parallel to the cliff-edge woods, with views to the east of Bossington Hill and Hurlstone Point on the far side of Porlock Bay.

Keep following this track, which keeps more or less parallel with the coast, crossing Holmer's Combe and Twitchin Combe, to Broomstreet Farm **7**. Keep to the seaward side of Broomstreet Farm through the farmyard and one or two gateways. The track soon turns to keep parallel with the coast. Keep on along this track until all trace of it disappears and there is open grassy field before you. Go into the field and turn immediately seawards to go through a gap at the lowest end. Make a steep descent to cross the stream and then keep seawards, rising slightly to the top of the steep western banks of Wheatham Combe. Continue seawards at the top of the steep slope and into the coastal woodland on the cliff slopes. The path turns westward, parallel to the sea which is some 650 feet (200 metres) below. This is Yenworthy Wood.

You soon emerge into open cliff slope meadows. Keep up and close to the stone-bank field boundary until it turns inland and up the hill. This point is called Guildhall Corner **8**. Now go away from the boundary and down hill at an angle. First of all the path descends gently through the grass between stunted larch and pine trees before an abrupt and well-worn descent westwards. The path then zigzags down to the main coast Path route. Turn right (east) if you are doing this walk as part of the round walk from Culbone or left (west) to continue towards Lynmouth.

route is well marked and makes for variety.

At Yenworthy wood the path keeps roughly level along the steep wooded coastal slopes. At the end of this a bridlegate gives access through a wall, where the path continues westwards briefly and then turn sharply inland at the corner of the wall to descend into Yenworthy Combe and cross the stream.

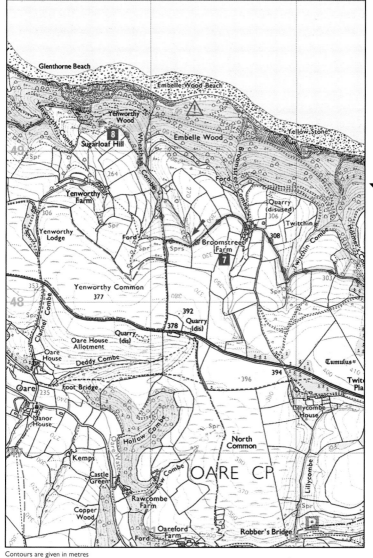

Contours are given in metres
The vertical interval is 10m

The steadily rising track emerges 400 yards (365 metres) west on a shoulder called Steeple Sturt **9**. Continue westwards and downhill through the woods, cross the stream at Coscombe, and then continue uphill on a forest track. Where this begins to level out look for a small flight of wooden steps on the right, which take the Coast Path seawards down to Sister's Fountain **10**, a small spring beneath a man-made cairn and rough-hewn slate cross.

Take the path that rises seawards from the fountain until you emerge on a track to pass between a pair of gate pillars surmounted by wild-boar heads. Go to the seaward side of the woodland lodge, dated 1853, with its ornate Victorian window tracery and barge-boards, and keep going along the track. Just before it turns sharply westward and downhill, the Coast Path mounts a low grassy bank to make its own way westwards towards Wingate Combe, keeping to the contours through the rhododendrons.

Lynton and Lynmouth from Countisbury. The earthworks on Wind Hill (centre left) are the remains of Iron Age coastal defences.

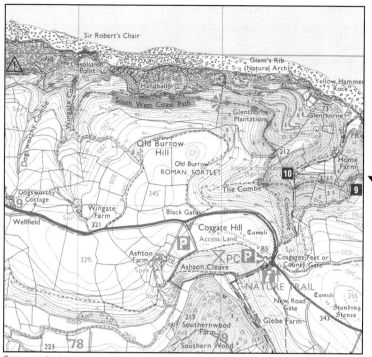

Contours are given in metres
The vertical interval is 10m

(If you are coming from the west, turn inland at this point, continue past the lodge of 1853, follow the small path left off the track just after the gates mentioned above, and then turn left and eastwards once you have passed Sister's Fountain **10**. The path now descends gently inland along its secure terrace to cross the stream of Wingate and return to the edge of the sea above Desolation Point. Still keeping level, the path turns due west to cross two more streams.)

Having gone round Wingate Combe, just beneath you and to your right you will see the rocky outcrop of Sir Robert's Chair. Beyond this point the path to the west has fallen away and so the route strikes diagonally uphill and inland for 30 or 40 yards on to a shoulder which separates the sea from the wooded banks of the stream flowing down from Desolate Farm. The path turns right (west) and continues up the crest of this shoulder.

(If you are coming from the west you will be able to look across the valley and see the path through the rhododendrons that brings you to the lodge above Sister's Fountain.)

The Lynmouth Cliff Railway. The weight of water in the tank of the downward car pulls the upward car to the top.

Continuing westwards, keep just to the seaward side of the shoulder, drop slightly to a small, dilapidated ruin, and then continue a steady descent, keeping parallel with the sea, to Pudleep Gurt **11** (one of a series of impressive miniature gorges). Swannelcombe **12** follows with a wealth of ferns, mosses and other greenery lining the tiny miniature waterfalls, followed by Chubhillcombe **13**.

Continue to the National Trust omega sign for Glenthorne Cliffs, go over the stile beside the gate, and follow the grassy track, still westwards, until you come to the lighthouse access road (single track) **C**. If you want to have a closer look at the lighthouse **14** (which was until recently open to the public, but is no longer), you can reach it by the access road, down through the centre of the dry valley, and then return on the same route to rejoin the Coast Path. The path marked on the map to the west of the lighthouse is unsafe.

(If you are coming from the west follow the lighthouse road eastwards and inland along Coddow Combe. Where the road comes to a hairpin bend carry on beside the dry stone wall until you come to the white gate mentioned above. Cross the stile next to it and look for the path, which rises on the bank straight ahead and is clearly defined through the woods and combes of Glenthorne.)

Continue down the lighthouse road and over the bridge **D**, and then immediately leave the road to turn away from the sea up a pleasant grassy track, which soon zigzags to the right (west) to follow the landward side of the scree-filled valley that dissects the Foreland.

You soon come into view of Lynmouth with its harbour, and Lynton above. You can see the water-powered cliff railway, which goes straight up the cliff behind Lynmouth harbour, and you have a good view of the coast beyond. In the foreground you can see the A39 Minehead–Lynton coast road. The Coast Path runs just below this almost all the way into Lynmouth, crosses the harbour, zigzags across the cliff railway, and then continues west halfway up the cliff slopes of Lynton.

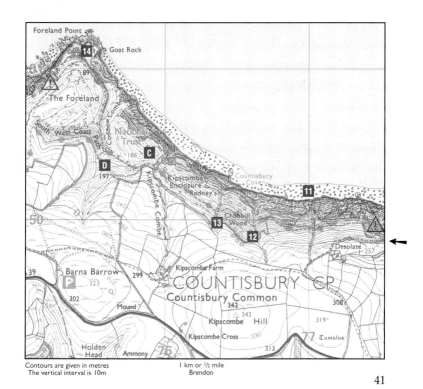

Contours are given in metres
The vertical interval is 10m

1 km or ½ mile
Brendon

Having come into view of Lynmouth, turn left (south-west) along the cliff top, past the gulley called Great Red and then keep to the grassy clifftop path along the edge of Butter Hill. Follow the field boundary stone wall and fence, keeping outside it until you are just below the main road. The substantial bank on the hillside is an Iron Age defensive earthwork.

The Coast Path continues just below the main road in a steady descent.

(If you are coming from the west and are presented with any forks on the path, take the higher one in each case.)

At a National Trust sign, which announces the western end of a 3-mile (5-km) stretch of the path owned by the Trust, you have to take to the road **E**, where there is no proper footway, for some

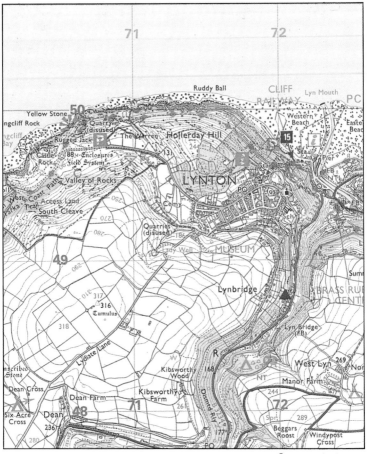

Contours are given in metres
The vertical interval is 10m

300 yards (275 metres). Turn seawards as soon as you find a well-defined path through a gap in the wall and go down the steep path through the woods, descending the hill in wide sweeping zigzags, taking the lower path where you have a choice, to descend parallel to the beach on the landward side of a sturdy stone wall. Make one final (right) seaward turn near the bottom, to emerge on a beach-side path leading straight towards Lynmouth harbour. Keep left of the Rock House Hotel where a footbridge will take you over to the harbour.

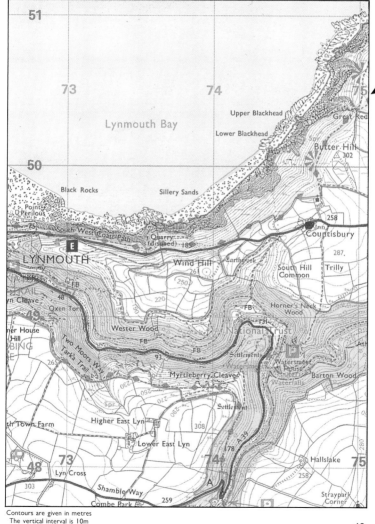

Contours are given in metres
The vertical interval is 10m

The Rhenish Tower at Lynmouth, now a popular tourist site, was originally a sea-water tower.

The smallest complete parish church in England is encountered at the village of Culbone.

Culbone Church

The main structure of Culbone Church **5** (see map on page 35) is probably 12th century with a 13th century chancel arch. You will find ancient oak pews, two small windows near the altar which may be Norman, and a 15th century rood screen.

Coleridge, Wordsworth, Byron and Southey in West Somerset

During the late 18th and early 19th centuries the therapeutic effect of wild landscapes such as Exmoor became a great attraction to the poets of the time. While staying in this area Coleridge wrote *The Rime of the Ancient Mariner* and when staying at an Exmoor farm on the coast of Somerset between Porlock and Lynton he wrote *Kubla Khan*.

The influence of the Exmoor landscape, the tiny church of Culbone on the steeply wooded slopes leading down to the sea and the wild cliffs of Exmoor can clearly be appreciated in *The Rime of the Ancient Mariner*. The ending of *Kubla Khan* was lost for ever to Coleridge's memory because a 'person from Porlock' called on business before he had finished writing it down.

Coleridge spent many days walking on Exmoor, sometimes accompanied by his brother-in-law Robert Southey. He was also friendly with Wordsworth, who lived for a time nearby on the Quantocks, and was an acquaintance of Byron, so there is a strong verbal tradition that Byron, too, was a visitor to Exmoor.

3 Lynmouth Harbour to Combe Martin

via Lynton and Martinhoe fortlet
12¾ miles (20.6 km)

Many of the buildings around the harbour at Lynmouth are new. On 15th August 1952, a cloudburst on Exmoor caused an unprecedented movement of boulders and tree trunks down to the river-bed in the village during the night, which led to a massive surge of water that washed away buildings and caused the death of thirty-four people.

From the harbour, zigzag up the hill behind the Rising Sun or, after visiting the Exmoor National Park Visitor Centre, go to the side of the information centre to follow a small zigzag path that also joins the North Walk. The cliff railway **15** was opened in 1890 and operates over a length of 900 feet (275 metres) at a

Castle Rock at Wringcliff Bay near Lynton. Wild goats often graze here, and round the corner is the famous Valley of Rocks.

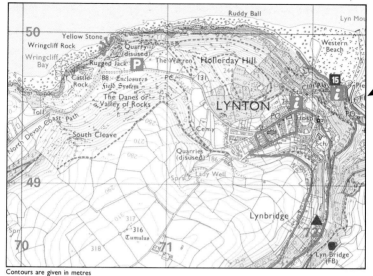

Contours are given in metres
The vertical interval is 10m

gradient steeper than one in two. It was partly financed by local resident Sir George Newnes of the publishing company. If you are feeling like a bit of fun, take a ride on it. It is driven by the weight of water in a tank of the down-coming car. When the car reaches the bottom, the water is emptied out and the car at the top has its tank filled until it starts its slow downward descent, pulling the other car to the top.

Having joined the North Walk, under water power or your own steam, so to speak, continue along it, around Hollerday Hill, to the Valley of the Rocks. Below the rocks called Rugged Jack you may see mountain goats clinging to the cliff edge. Looking west across Lee Bay and Woody Bay, the headland in the distance is Highveer Point with the Cow and Calf headland a little nearer, and Wringapeak on the other side of Woody Bay.

Soon you round a corner and see ahead of you Wringcliff Bay with Castle Rock towering above it, and Duty Point Tower, a folly on the headland east of Lee Bay. Go to the landward side of Castle Rock. After this the Coast Path follows the road.

(If you are coming from the west you will see a roundabout ahead of you. Towering above this roundabout is Castle Rock to the west and Rugged Jack to the east. Between the two you will see a tarmac path leading round to the north of Rugged Jack. Follow this all the way to Lynton where, at its easternmost end, it zigzags down to the harbour.)

Continuing west, the Coast Path leaves the road after $1\frac{1}{2}$ miles (2.4 km) and goes seawards into the woods, 200 yards (180 metres) after you have left the turning to Slattenslade on your landward side.

The track through the woods crosses a small bridge over a tumbling stream. Soon after passing a house you come on to a surfaced road, officially a public bridleway, which you follow westward. Looking east, you can now see Crock Point across Woody Bay to Duty Point and its folly. This track reaches a hairpin bend **A** towards the western end of Woody Bay. On the corner of the bend is a gate. Go through this and continue westwards along a forest track.

As you come out of Woodybay Wood you will see ahead of you the massive steep slopes leading up towards the Roman fortlet **16** mentioned on page 56, and round the next corner you will see a magnificent waterfall, the sort you can stand under to get cool on a hot day. This is Hollow Brook, which issues from a spring just above Martinhoe. Note the masses of ramsons (wild garlic) and their characteristic smell. Looking back east you will now see the cave at Wringapeak which has pierced right through the headland, letting the sea surge through from both directions, to dramatic effect during stormy weather.

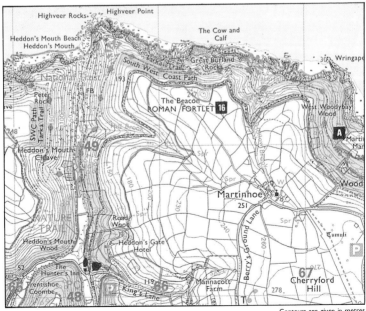

Contours are given in metres
The vertical interval is 10m

You will soon be looking down on the mouth of the River Heddon. The circular building you can see is one of the lime kilns, once supplied with coal and limestone shipped into Heddon's Mouth from South Wales.

The path now turns inland and downwards until it joins the Riverside Walk towards the Hunter's Inn. Just upstream from this point there is a new bridge that you cross, briefly going downstream on the western side to join a track on the other side, then continuing upstream again.

Look out for a small path through the woodland to the right, which rises back towards the coast. Continue in this direction until you come out of the woods and into a steep, dry valley covered in bracken, silver birch and hawthorn. Here the Coast Path zigzags in wide sweeps until halfway up, at about 330 feet (100 metres), where it once again turns seawards right across the dry valley.

The narrow grassy path continues coastwards to Peter Rock overlooking the treacherous rocks at the mouth of the River Heddon. Continue west from Peter Rock on a well-made but narrow path that follows the very steep upper slopes of the cliffs. First keeping level and then rising, a distinctive slate-surfaced track just under a yard wide traverses heather-covered

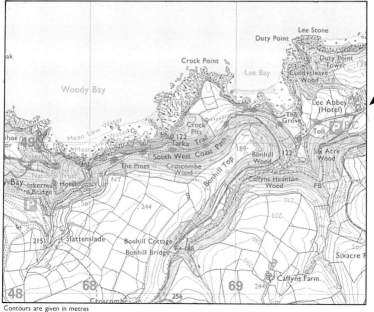

Contours are given in metres
The vertical interval is 10m

49

The Coast Path at Heddon's Mouth Cleave near Hunter's Inn.

slopes with outcrops of jagged slate and some scree. After one more steep rise around East Cleave a magnificent view of the cliffs to the west opens up. Here the path turns briefly south to reach the top of the coastal slopes and then follows the distinctive Devon stone and earth field boundary at the top of these clifftop slopes.

You will see Neck Wood just below you to the west and the heights of Trentishoe Down and Holdstone Down to the southwest, each around 1,000 feet (300 metres) high. You do not have to reach the top of either of them! Just before the deep gulley east of Neck Wood, turn into the field (where all the old boundaries have recently been removed) and make your way round the back of the coastal hollows, by and large keeping your height as you do so. At the far western end you will find a stile and gate that lets you out on to the unenclosed National Trust land. Follow the well-defined stony track due west, rising steadily until you come to a stone and earth boundary. Pass through the gap in the boundary and you will see small circular humps, hollow in the middle, about 10–15 yards inland of the Coast Path. These are Bronze Age hut circles **17**, the dwellings of the inhabitants of Trentishoe some 3,000 years ago.

(If you are coming from the west, cross the field, making for the clifftop stile, then follow the field boundary on the cliff side until it turns abruptly inland. This is East Cleave and, by following the distinctive path on a ledge around the upper part of the steep slopes near Heddon's Mouth, you will soon reach Heddon's Mouth Cleave, the dry valley through which the path zigzags down to the River Heddon. On reaching the river, go briefly downstream, cross the bridge, and join the footpath that rises steadily on the other side of Heddon's Mouth (eastern side). Then continue until you come out on to the lane to the Valley of the Rocks. There, take the path towards the cliffs, keep going eastwards, and you will emerge near the head of the cliff railway at Lynton.)

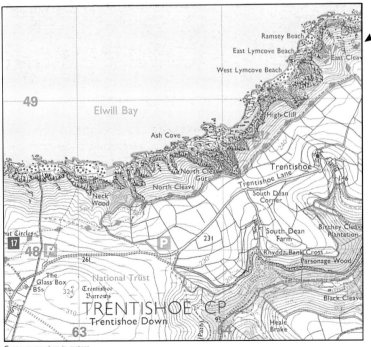

Contours are given in metres
The vertical interval is 10m

Trentishoe and Holdstone Downs, with the Great Hangman beyond.

You soon join a wide grassy track leading down from the coast road. Looking across the Bristol Channel, you are now due south of the Mumbles, with Swansea and Port Talbot steelworks to the right and the Gower peninsula to the left.

The track begins to descend gently and passes through the centre of some partially improved sheep pasture, after which it arrives at a substantial stone and earth field boundary overlooking Sherrycombe. Follow this field boundary inland for a hundred yards and then pass through it to follow the western (lower) side inland for a further 200 yards (180 metres) and you will see a group of farm buildings, Holdstone Farm. Branch down at 45 degrees from the field boundary, still heading inland but gradually descending into the valley of Sherrycombe. Downhill and ahead you will see the National Trust sign for the 'Great Hangman'. Cross the stile and continue down towards the stream. On the far side of the valley you will see the Coast Path rising steadily in a seaward direction across the western side of the combe.

(If you are coming from the west, take the diagonal path sloping down into Sherrycombe, go straight up the hill opposite, through the National Trust boundary, then keep left, seawards, gradually bearing round towards the east along the broad track mentioned above.)

Travelling west, you will now approach the heights of Girt (Great) Down. Keep up the path until it comes close to a substantial field boundary corner. Turn left (west), keeping parallel to the cliffs. At the end of the wall, fork slightly seawards up a broad track going north-west. Make for a cairn ahead, which marks the summit of the Great Hangman at 1,043 feet (318 metres) the highest point on the South West Coast Path. The name may have nothing to do with capital punishment or sheep stealing. The second part of the name relates to the Celtic word for hill (*mynedd*) and *Hang* is the germanic word for slope – the sloping hill – as in the Old Man of Hoy or East Man and West Man in Purbeck. The pure Celtic base of the languages still spoken in Brittany, Ireland and Scotland bears no derivation from any other European language, having a common root only in Sanskrit. This is almost certainly why the Latin word for hill (*mons, montis*) bears similarities to the Celtic word *mynedd* (pronounced 'muneth'), giving us two good reasons why a hill might end up with the name 'man'.

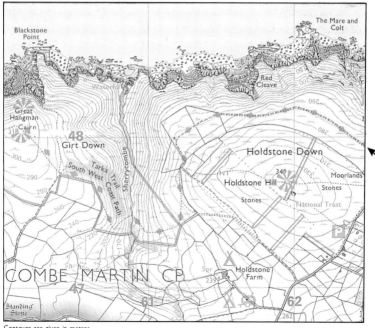

Contours are given in metres
The vertical interval is 10m

Ahead of you lies Combe Martin Bay with the pyramidal shape of Little Hangman in the foreground. Go straight towards Little Hangman, following the ridge, until you come to a fence, turn very briefly seawards and follow this fence on the seaward side. Go through a kissing gate and down some wooden steps, still keeping outside the fields and at the top of the cliff slopes. Just before you reach the Little Hangman cross a stile. The Coast Path skirts round the inland side of the Little Hangman until it directly overlooks Combe Martin Bay. Now follow the clifftop slopes, keeping outside the fence around the back of Wild Pear Beach.

The Coast Path continues along the top of the cliff just inside a hedge, and views of Combe Martin Church soon open up. In spring, herb robert, campion, ground ivy, bluebells, primroses, violets, foxgloves, celandines and wood-sage line the clifftop path, which soon rises to look back at the Little Hangman with the moorland top of Great Hangman on the horizon. This is Lester Cliff. Continue westwards to a rain shelter. Just past the rain shelter the official route goes left into Combe Martin behind a row of houses. You may prefer to stay near the clifftop and cross the lawns that lead down towards the shingle beach. Little can be detected of the small fishing settlement that must once have been associated with this fine natural harbour. Combe Martin is now predominantly an Edwardian village and apart from the ugly clifftop caravans, which are mainly visible only from the Coast Path, it is now a quiet and pleasant resort.

One small piece of evidence of a former trade with South Wales is the name of the car park – the Kiln car park. Cross this car park, passing the Exmoor National Park and Tourist Information Centre.

The mines of Combe Martin

There is a legend that there was a trade in silver and lead from the Combe Martin mines to the Mediterranean by visiting Phoenician merchants, and we know that the mines were in full operation in the late 13th century. The silver probably enabled the English to pay for their escapades in France, at Crécy, Poitiers and Agincourt. They closed 150 years ago.

Contours are given in metres
The vertical interval is 10m

A circular walk to Martinhoe Roman fortlet

5 miles (8 km)

This walk starts from the Hunter's Inn (National Trust car park, grid ref. SS655 482). Go to the right (east) of the pub following the upper route towards the sea. This path rises gradually, branching east round a steep valley, and continues north-west and seawards to join the crest of the clifftop slopes, going east. When you see a seat beside the path you are close to the Martinhoe Roman fortlet **16**, at a height of just under 800 feet (245 metres). Here you will see a series of concentric earth rings, and excavations revealed two blocks of barrack buildings which housed about 80 Roman soldiers. The lookout was built to keep an eye on the inhabitants of Wales, the Silures, around AD 59.

To continue round the circular walk, just follow the track eastwards until you come to West Woodybay Wood, where it turns south to follow the edge of the wood. After 545 yards (500 metres) you will come to a junction where you turn left and seawards to join the Coast Path. Follow this route, which is well defined, west past the waterfall to Heddon's Mouth. Follow the Coast Path inland to a bridge over the River Heddon. Here you continue upstream until you reach the Hunter's Inn again.

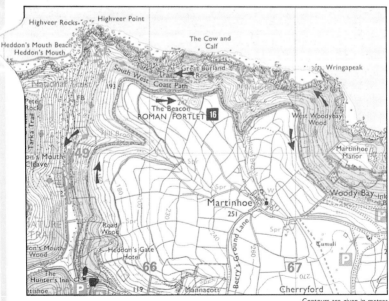

Contours are given in metres
The vertical interval is 10m

The coast at Martinhoe, looking east across Woody Bay and Lee Bay to The Foreland at Countisbury.

4 Combe Martin to Mortehoe and Woolacombe

including Lundy Island
13 miles (20.8 km)

Follow the coast road west up the hill and around the corner above the beach. Just before the main road straightens out, a narrow tarmac lane leads seawards. Go along this lane, past the former parish boundary marker between Combe Martin and Berrynarbor, and sharp right up a sunken lane. This lane rejoins the main road **A** to follow the footway that runs parallel with it. In due course this footway returns to the old road by a wooden ladder.

Turn left and then right to follow the new A399 coastal road west for about 400 yards (365 metres) until you reach the crest of a hill. Here, a Coast Path sign on your right takes you onto a quiet lane leading to the Sandycove Hotel. Keeping just to the landward side of the hotel follow the old coast road, which soon becomes a beech-lined track, north-westwards. Follow the track until you see a drive entering from the landward side. Here the Coast Path leaves the track to go seawards over wooden steps.

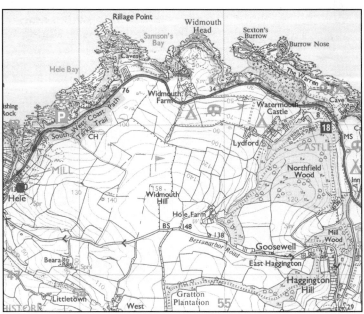

Contours are given in metres
The vertical interval is 10m

You are now looking into a fine miniature natural harbour called Water Mouth. The Coast Path follows the seaward side of the next two fields, the lower of which is a camping field in summer, returning to the main road near Watermouth Castle **18**, built in the Gothic style in 1825, possibly on older foundations, and now an entertainment centre.

Normally you should be able to follow the edge of Water Mouth but, if the tide is very high, follow the road a short distance west and take the stile into the sycamore wood with its bluebells, primroses and campion, to rejoin the Coast Path.

As the path comes out of the woods keep to the seaward side of the meadow. The headland is called Widmouth and you are soon standing just under the old coastguard lookout hut with a view of Lundy Island (see pages 66 and 68) due west above the caves of Rillage Point, the coast of Wales to the north, and the high rugged cliffs of Exmoor to the east. As you come round from Widmouth Head into Samson's Bay, notice the fulmars gliding around their nesting area on the cliffs.

After Widmouth Head the path goes to the back of Samson's Bay. Turn right (west) sharply as you come within sight of Widmouth Farm. Keep on along the cliff top to Rillage Point. From here you can see Ilfracombe just $1\frac{1}{4}$ miles (2 km) ahead. From Rillage Point the Coast Path returns to run alongside the coast road, partly on a separate path and partly on the verge, until it reaches a picnic area. Follow the pavement down into Hele, turn right (seawards) at the Hele Bay Hotel, go down to the beach, and then up the steps to the seaward side of the toilets.

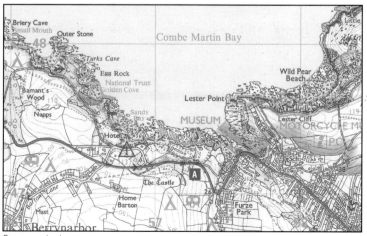

Contours are given in metres
The vertical interval is 10m

Sunset behind Lantern Hill and St Nicholas Chapel, Ilfracombe.

Zigzag up the hill, observing any diversion signs necessitated by recent cliff falls. Nearly at the top you will see some iron railings, from where there is a fine view over Ilfracombe and Lundy Island. The Coast Path now returns inland for a hundred yards or so, and turns westwards again as you come once more into full view of Ilfracombe. The massive ramparts here are the remains of the double-banked Iron Age promontory fort of Hillsborough. Make your way into the town across the open public spaces before you. You may wish to explore the pleasant harbour and visit the lifeboat house and St Nicholas Chapel **19** and lighthouse. Town trail leaflets are available from the Tourist Information Centre.

On entering Ilfracombe Harbour, look for the blue street tile signs to guide you through the town. To leave the harbour turn left into Hierns Lane and then right into Broad Street. Continue towards the quay for 150 yards, then turn left into Capstone Road keeping the public house on your right.

At the end of Capstone Road turn right along Capstone Parade. On reaching Wildersmouth Beach, at the end of Capstone Parade, aim for the New Landmark Theatre (a new, futuristic looking building.) Take the steps beside this building and follow the path up onto Granville Road. Turn right and follow this road until you reach a turning on your right which is Torrs Walk Avenue. Look for the Coast Path sign for Torrs Walk and Lee.

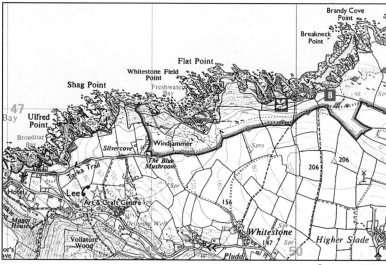

Contours are given in m
The vertical interval is

Continuing west, go seawards from the National Trust sign for a 220-yard (200-metre) walk along the cliff edge, before zigzagging up the Seven Hills southwards, going right (west) at a junction on the way up.

Bull Point and the lighthouse buildings have now come into sight to the west with Lundy in the background. When you reach the Seven Hills, go a little way inland and join the clearly defined grass track west, which goes to the seaward side of the highest bumps. When you see a fence ahead of you **B**, turn inland until you come to a stile and then turn once again westwards to follow what is now a farm track but used to be the old coast road from Ilfracombe to Lee.

Keep to the farm track west until, near some bungalows, it becomes a lane which takes you all the way to Lee. Once there, follow the road round the back of the beach and west up the hill.

(If you are coming from the west, take the road round the back of the beach and go behind the Lee Bay Hotel. At the back of the hotel building you will see a steep lane rising left (east) – this is the Coast Path to Ilfracombe.)

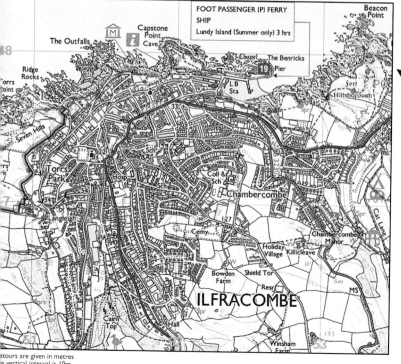

tours are given in metres
e vertical interval is 10m

Going west from Lee Bay, climb up the road until you come to a National Trust sign for Damage Hue. Go through the wicket gate, right (west), and follow the cliff top. The prehistoric standing stones **20** shown on the map are likely to have been religious monuments during the Early Bronze Age.

Between here and Bull Point **21** the Path dips to sea level and twice rises again to over 200 feet (60 metres). The path is well defined and provided with steps in the steeper places. When you see the lighthouse at Bull Point, first constructed in 1879 and often open in the afternoons to visitors, make for the landward side of the enclosure, cross the lighthouse road and continue south-west. The path crosses a grassy area before zigzagging up among some small cliffs, after which it continues, for 1¼ miles (2 km), all the way along the cliff top to Morte Point.

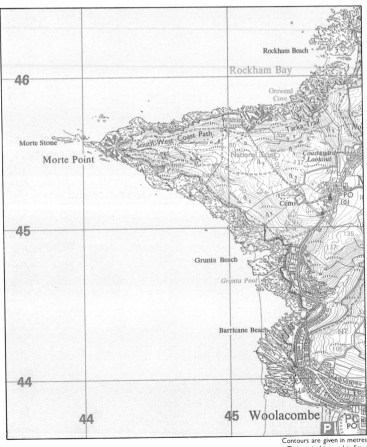

Contours are given in metres
The vertical interval is 5m

On the way, you must wind in and out among little knolls before dropping down to Rockham Beach, where you may see your first seal. You may also hear the rattling noise of the tiny whitethroat and see it hopping among the gorse bushes.

After passing Whiting Cove, the Coast Path rises briefly to a seat, before descending again westwards to follow the lower part of the cliff slopes towards Morte Point. As you round Morte Point heading for Woolacombe, the coast of Wales disappears and a new view opens up of virtually the whole of the rest of the North Devon coast. In the foreground is the wide sweep of Woolacombe Sand and Morte Bay with Baggy Point in the middle distance. Mortehoe and Woolacombe have pleasant accommodation, and Mortehoe Church, of Norman origin, has some interesting features, including medieval bench-ends.

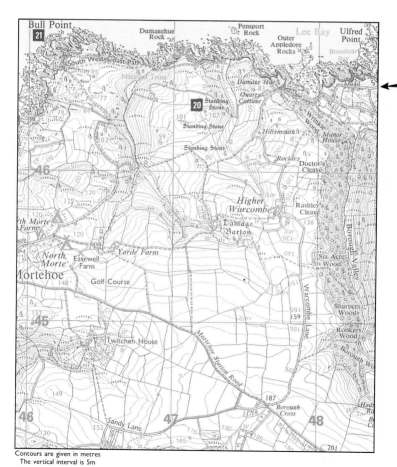

Contours are given in metres
The vertical interval is 5m

A CIRCULAR WALK ON LUNDY ISLAND

4½ miles (7.4 km)

If you study the timetables carefully you may manage to spend five to six hours on this island. To give yourself time to explore, it will be best to do this circuit of the southern half of the island.

From the landing beach, head up the steep track to the Marisco Tavern, where you can buy guide books and maps. Then take the left-hand route heading south past the church of St Helena, built in the 1800s when the island was owned by the Rev. Heaven and known locally as the kingdom of Heaven. Make for Marisco Castle, originally built for Henry III in 1240 but now a holiday cottage. Here you overlook the southern lighthouse, built on a slate promontory which juts out from this granite island.

From the castle turn west to follow the impressive 400-foot (120-metre) cliffs until you come to the old lighthouse, built in 1897 on the highest point. It was abandoned because low cloud or sea fog rendered it too often ineffective. Now head north-west across the high, flat plateau of the island to Battery Point, and there take the narrow track from the cliff top down to a deserted cottage and a building in which two cannon were once placed, giving this headland its name.

Now retrace your steps to the cliff top, and continue north to Jenny's Cove, past the mysterious cracks in the cliff top attributed to an earthquake which hit Lisbon in Portugal in the 1750s. Then turn right and inland (east) up Punchbowl Valley to the man-made Pondsbury pond. The fringes of the pond provide the habitat for a variety of beautiful small plants, including the yellow bog asphodel and the red insectivorous sundew.

From Pondsbury, head north-east past the remains of a wartime Heinkel bomber, and then turn right (south) on to the track along the eastern side of the island. The track was a railway built to carry the granite which was used all over the Empire.

The track hugs the cliff side. Seals are regular visitors and these waters are rich in marine wildlife. Unpolluted, sheltered and fed by the Atlantic and the Gulf Stream, these waters were designated as Britain's first statutory marine nature reserve.

On passing the large netted area, a 'Heligoland' bird trap, used to help record migratory birds, follow the tunnel through the rhododendrons back to the Mill Coombe Hotel and thence, depending on the time left, retire to the Marisco Tavern or turn left and return to the landing beach.

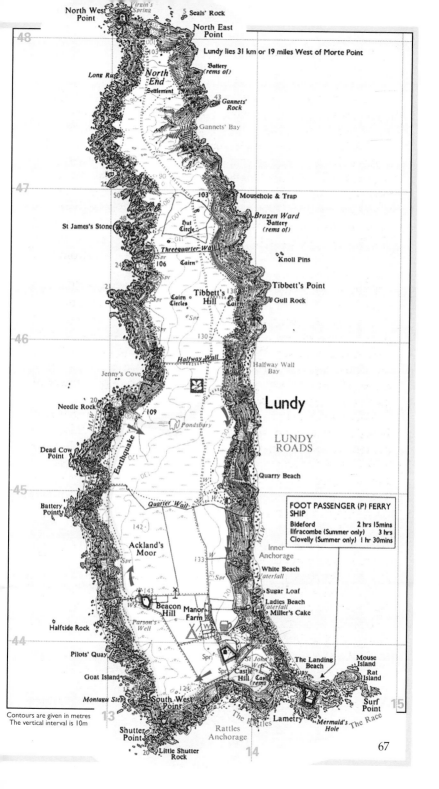

Contours are given in metres
The vertical interval is 10m

67

Lundy Island

This three-mile-long island, whose name derives from the Norse for puffin, can often be visited for the day from Ilfracombe or Bideford. Consult the timetables available from a local tourist information centre listed at the back of this book. Since 1969 the island has been owned by the National Trust who have leased it to the Landmark Trust. (Booking details for camping or accommodation: The Landmark Trust, Shottesbrooke, Maidenhead, Berkshire, tel. 01628 825925. Book well ahead if you have to go during the school holidays.) The sailing schedules and choice of departure ports are based on tides, as is the amount of time that day visitors have to explore the island. You may like to aim for a date when there is plenty of time to explore the dramatic cliff scenery of the island, and remember that the puffins, razorbills and guillemots are normally in residence only from spring until late June or early July.

You will land on the beach at the south of the island and can start exploring there (see page 66 for a circular walk). There are the ruins of Marisco Castle, the old lighthouse, and 7 miles (11.25 km) of coastline, including 400-foot (120-metre) cliffs, with views of the coasts of Devon (of which Lundy is officially part), Cornwall, Pembrokeshire and Glamorgan.

Walker's footsteps at Woolacombe Sand, looking back towards Mortehoe.

5 Mortehoe and Woolacombe to Braunton

around Baggy Point
16 miles (25.7 km)

(Altogether the route around the Taw and Torridge Estuaries that follow requires some 20 miles (32 km) of flat walking through dunes and along dykes and railway lines beside a tame estuarine landscape. It is pleasant walking and good for outings on foot or by bicycle. Also, it is essential to complete it if you are determined to cover the whole trail. If, however, you came for the wild cliff scenery, you may decide to catch a bus from Saunton, which has several buses a day, or Braunton, which has a 15-minute service to Westward Ho!, changing at Barnstaple.)

As you approach the centre of Woolacombe from Mortehoe and see a car park and phone boxes on your right, take the road going right (west) and follow it, leaving the beach access to your right (unless you plan to walk across the sands to Putsborough). Ignore any small paths that lead into the sand dunes on the right and continue until you come to a Coast Path sign pointing right along a bridleway. Take this path and follow the waymarks through the sand dunes.

Stay within the flat area behind the dunes for a while and, where a more pronounced dip begins **A**, branch uphill and inland. When you come to a fork where a rather eroded path descends into the dunes once more **B**, make your way uphill towards an old quarry to join the Marine Drive.

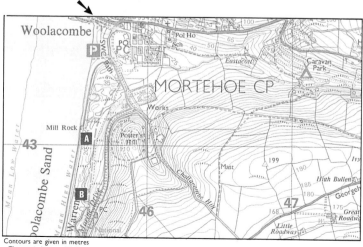

Contours are given in metres
The vertical interval is 5m

The Coast Path keeps to the well-defined track, passing to the landward side of the settlement of Vention and the car park and caravan site there. Look across at the Baggy Point peninsula, so that you can work out your route to Baggy Point along the top of the cliff slopes.

Now keep straight ahead, to the landward side of the holiday flats and along the county road, for a further 200 yards (180 metres), before turning right (west) at a gateway with a stile beside it.

Follow the track beside the field boundary until you reach the top of the steeper slope and then branch about 20 degrees to the right until you come to the gorse-covered slopes. The Coast Path stays at the top of these slopes, meandering in and out of the gorse in places.

From Baggy Point you can enjoy one of the closest views you will get of Lundy Island (see pages 66 and 68). Looking almost due north across the rocks off Morte Point you may see Swansea and the Gower peninsula. With good binoculars and on a very

Contours are given in metres
The vertical interval is 5m

clear day, you will be able to make out the smoking chimneys of the Milford Haven oil refineries and the cliffs of Pembrokeshire.

From the southern side of Baggy Point you can see what lies ahead on the route, with Bideford Bay in the foreground. From Westward Ho! to Hartland Point, where you may see the lighthouse flashing, is all unspoilt coastline. Halfway along you may be able to identify Buck's Mills nestling in a small combe beside the sea and, slightly to the right of centre, Clovelly. The Coast Path stays more or less on the cliff top for the whole of that stretch.

To continue on the Coast Path, go to the extreme south-west corner of Baggy Point, cross a stile, and follow the yard-wide stone path that starts down the cliff towards the point and then turns sharply back towards Croyde Bay (see page 72) to continue on the level along the coastal slope.

Keep straight on down this path, which becomes the village street. Continue past the National Trust car park and along the lane until you see a sign to the beach. Turn right (south), make

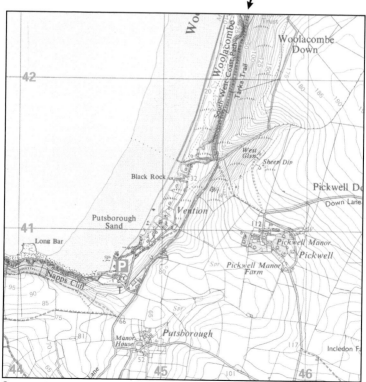

Contours are given in metres
The vertical interval is 5m

71

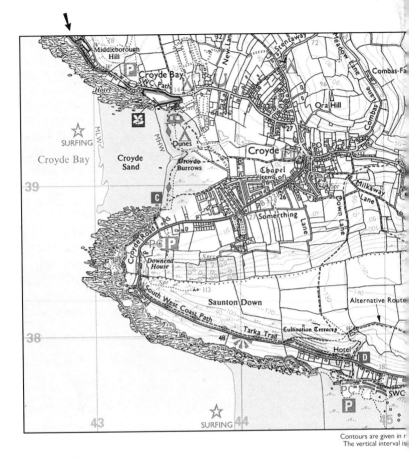

Contours are given in r
The vertical interval is

your way on to the beach and towards the far southern corner. The official route goes along the base of the dunes over a bridge, but I found it easier to keep to the hard sand by the water.

At the southernmost end you will see a flight of steps leaving the beach: these are private. Make for a wartime blockhouse and turn right **C** (west), walking along a line of rocks just under the cliff. Continue under the cliff across one tiny sandy beach, and the path climbs to the cliff top via another flight of steps. Turn right to continue along the low grassy cliff until Saunton Sands come into sight. Make for the old coastguard lookout above you, where you have to cross the main road by turning left and then right to rejoin the path, which rises up some concrete steps before turning right (south), and continues above and parallel to the main coast road.

Before you descend to the main road at the Saunton Sands Hotel look south at the Braunton Burrows sand dunes, a national nature reserve. On the main road there is a bus stop **D** for the Croyde–Saunton–Barnstaple buses, which you may wish to take if river estuaries and sand dunes do not appeal as much as the rugged cliffs. As you approach the main road, you have a choice. An alternative footpath route has been provided over Saunton Down which avoids a road section. Turn left inland up a steep slope to the top of the hill. At the top turn right and pass behind an old ruined building. Follow the track along the ridge and descend the hill towards Braunton. Follow the track down past Saunton Court where it becomes a surfaced road; keeping right, rejoin the main Coast Path by crossing the road at the crossroads.

The official route loops round the landward side of the Saunton Sands Hotel and follows a track south of the houses on the coast road. It then joins the main road for 330 yards (300 metres) to Saunton, taking the first turning right after the golf course entrance.

Where this lane turns a sharp corner, carry straight on

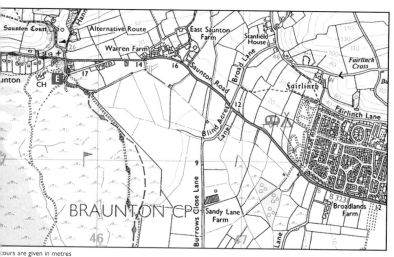

ours are given in metres
vertical interval is 10m

through a wicket gate **E**, across the field, and through a bridle gate, which takes you on to the golf course. Turn left (south-east) down the broad sandy bridleway past a red-tiled barn and keep to this sandy track as it continues south. When the track becomes less well defined, bear briefly left to avoid the green ahead of you, and then continue south with a thicket separating the path from grazing land on the landward side.

The path continues in the same general direction through thickets, winding its way rather more than the definitive line of the map would indicate.

As you enter Braunton Burrows Nature Reserve there is also a Ministry of Defence ranges sign, warning you not to pass when the red flag is flying. (Enquiries tel. 01271 375101 extn. 3536. Exercises, 30 days per annum only, are also advertised in local press.)

Provided it is safe to proceed, carry straight on south until reaching a T-junction with a stone track **F**. Turn left (inland) and you will come in a few yards to a car park with an information board. The boundaries of both the nature reserve and the army danger area are indicated on the maps.

When you reach a parking area **G** at the end of the track you can follow a board walk west, still through sand dunes, to look at the mouth of the River Taw, before retracing your steps to the car park. The Coast Path continues east along another broad stone track with low marshy meadows on the left and bramble-covered dunes on the right.

Looking across the Taw and Torridge Estuaries to Appledore from Braunton Burrows Nature Reserve.

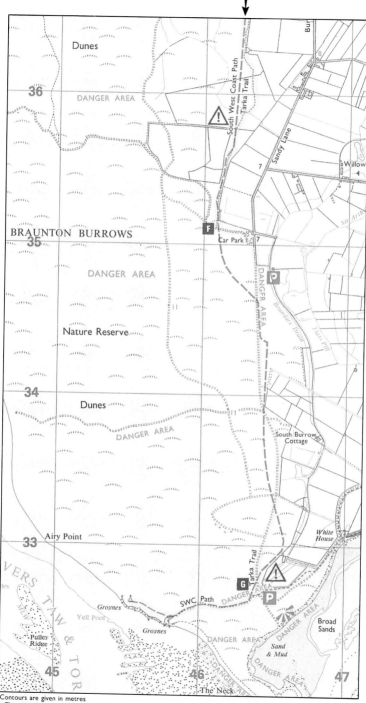

Contours are given in metres
The vertical interval is 5m

Banks of the River Taw Estuary at the White House, Braunton Burrows.

You soon come to White House, where the track becomes a surfaced toll road heading north, and the Coast Path turns right and then left along the dyke beside the estuary all the way to Braunton, 2½ miles (4 km) away.

When the riverside walk finishes, take the road until you see the former level-crossing **H** of the old Ilfracombe–Barnstaple railway, which is now the Coast Path.

Braunton's 13th century church is well worth a visit. There is accommodation in the centre of the village which can be reached by turning left (north) at the level-crossing **H**. In the Caen Field car park the Braunton Countryside Centre has exhibitions about the area's attractions, such as the Great Field. The Tourist Information Centre and museum are in the same car park. Braunton Great Field, 350 acres (142 hectares) of medieval open-field system, is still in cultivation in the traditional fashion.

(If you are coming from Barnstaple into Braunton along the railway track, go to the first level-crossing **H** and turn left (south). Then look for the access to the banks of the stream. Follow the dyke for about an hour and join the bridleway by White House. Follow that bridleway through the nature reserve and the golf course, cross the coast road, and follow the Coast Path above it to Croyde.)

The Barnstaple to Ilfracombe Railway

The Coast Path from Braunton to Barnstaple, which is also a very good cycleway, is the former Barnstaple to Ilfracombe Railway. In 1870, the Barnstaple and Ilfracombe Railway Company obtained permission to build the line. Four years later the line was completed despite the challenges presented by the steep hills and valleys. The line was originally single track, then doubled and finally became a single line before closure.

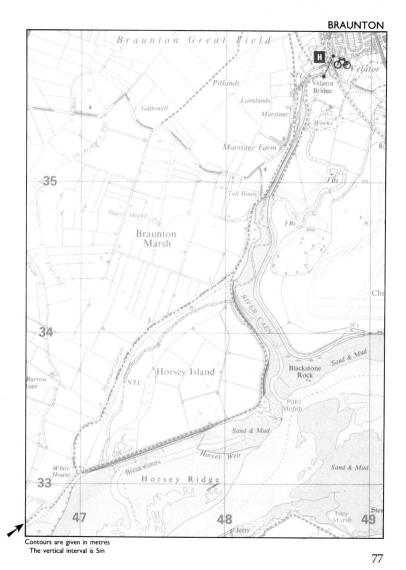

Contours are given in metres
The vertical interval is 5m

Riverside walk and the 15th century bridge at Barnstaple.

6 Braunton to Westward Ho!

via Bideford and Appledore
23 miles (37.0 km)

From Braunton, if you are starting a section of the walk here, go down South Street and continue until you see the level-crossing **H**. Continue past Signal Court on your right before you join the old railway track and walk for 5 miles (8 km) to Barnstaple up one side of the estuary. After that you will go the same distance back down the other side to Instow, where there is sometimes a ferry in high season when tides permit. Otherwise continue a further 3 miles (5 km) up the Torridge Estuary to Bideford Bridge and back down the estuary to Appledore. There are frequent buses (Barnstaple to Ilfracombe) (tel. 01271 345444) at approximate 15-minute intervals from 7 a.m. until 6 p.m. All these buses also stop at Chivenor, and there are equally frequent services to Westward Ho! from Barnstaple. You may decide to walk part and bus part of the way.

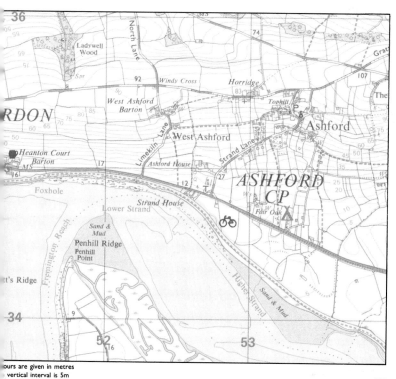

ours are given in metres
vertical interval is 5m

Assuming that you are walking from Braunton, as you approach Barnstaple you will see some rugby grounds on your landward side and a few yards later you come within sight of Barnstaple Bridge. Bear away from the river, pass close to the rugby ground grandstand, and go down a narrow passageway past an agricultural engineering depot. Turn right across the front of the entrance of the engineering and county council depots and then turn right again as soon as you can into a lane that leads to Rolle Quay. Looking across the quay you will see a knoll with trees on it. This was the castle mound where a fortified stone castle was built in the 12th century. The tourist information centre is in the library nearby. The Pannier Market, a remnant of Barnstaple's heyday as a market town, is still used for markets on Tuesdays and Fridays. John Gay, poet, dramatist and author of *The Beggar's Opera*, went to school in Barnstaple. The Guildhall was built in 1826 in the Grecian style and is sometimes open for visits, and there are other historical curiosities worth inspecting if you have a little time to spare.

To continue west, follow the quayside signs and cross the 15th century Long Bridge, taking the first turning right. Keep the industrial buildings on your right and houses on your left and go down a gravel track past bollards. Ahead you will soon

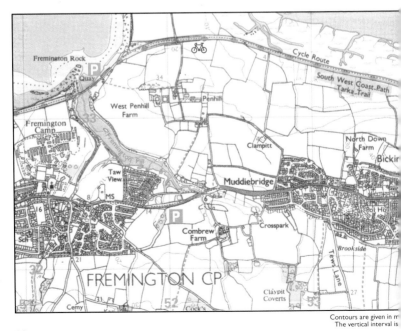

Contours are given in m
The vertical interval is

see two railway bridges where the functioning railway now ends and the rest of the track has become the Coast Path to Bideford. Get on to the track and follow it.

After 2½ miles (4 km) you will see a quay adjoining the railway line. Go over a railway bridge across the small creek. If you decide to take a bus from Fremington, go south from the further (western) side of the bridge and follow a footpath which leaves the beach almost immediately (do not follow the beach for any distance, since there is no public way out at the end). Follow this path into Fremington where you will be able to pick up the very frequent bus service between Barnstaple and Westward Ho!

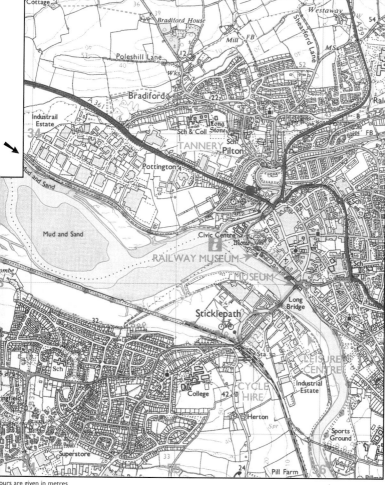

ours are given in metres
vertical interval is 5m

Continue along the railway track from Fremington to Instow, passing Home Farm Marsh and Instow Barton Marsh.

Between April and September, inclusive, there is a ferry from Instow to Appledore, 2 hours before and after high tide only, enabling you to take a shortcut, although you will miss Bideford town if you do. To take the ferry turn right off the railway track by the signal box at Instow and follow the riverside road for 200 yards to The Quay. On reaching the other side of the river follow the road right (north) to West Appledore.

You can also complete the last 2½ miles (4 km) to The Quay by turning right off the railway line at East Yelland Marsh.

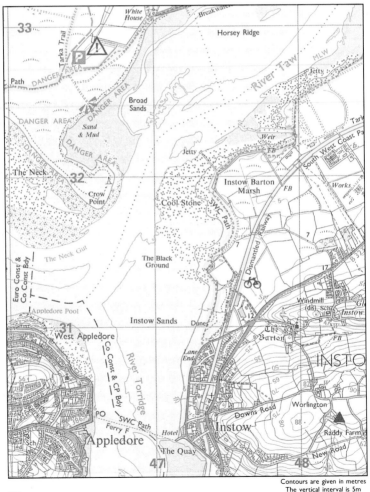

Contours are given in metres
The vertical interval is 5m

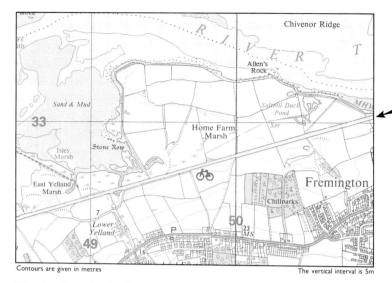

Contours are given in metres   The vertical interval is 5m

The view from the old Barnstaple–Bideford Railway (part of the Tarka Trail).

83

The Coast Path from Lynton to Bideford is part of the Tarka Trail. The 180-mile (300-km) trail makes use of part of the former Bideford–Okehampton railway following Tarka the otter's journeys along the River Torridge, with a southern link into Dartmoor and a return to Barnstaple down the Taw Valley. Bideford Station now has some old rolling stock and a Tarka Trail Visitor Centre is being developed.

At Bideford, leave the railway and cross the bridge, then turn right (north) along Bideford Quay. Keep as close to the river as you can, going straight ahead at the small roundabout on the new housing estate to go under the new A39 bridge. Keep straight ahead past a cottage and alongside a high stone wall before turning back to the river along a narrow stone-wall-bordered passage. At the river's edge turn left (north) along the top of a low cliff. This takes you in front of a pleasant group of Victorian-style villas and past an old quay **A**.

When you see an array of 'private' and house name signs in front of you **B**, take the middle path, which branches away from the river. Cross the valley past a small well and then go up the hill between tank traps, before turning back towards the river and the riverside National Trust property of Burrough Farm.

By a house **C** further along the river bank you now have a choice at low tide. Either you can follow the dike along the shoreline or you can go inland over a stile and continue up a house drive for some 200 yards (180 metres) before turning right (north) once again. Follow the landward side of the old hedge boundary before turning right (north-east) across a stream. Now go towards the river until you see a wooden stile in a stone wall. Cross this and follow the fence around the landward side of the shipyard (marked as 'works' on the map), turning right (west) to Appledore. *If you have any doubts about the state of the tide or the flow of water through the hole in the dike, use the inland alternative.* A visit to the museum at Appledore is recommended.

(If you are leaving Appledore for Bideford, follow the road south, parallel to the River Torridge. Where this turns inland, follow it to the works entrance and take the path just beyond it. Turn away from the river as you leave the barbed-wire enclosure until you cross a small stream. Turn left (south) and follow the inland side of the hedge there to the drive. Go seawards to rejoin the original route. Keep near the river to Bideford Bridge. Then mount the steps to follow the old railway track to Barnstaple and Braunton.)

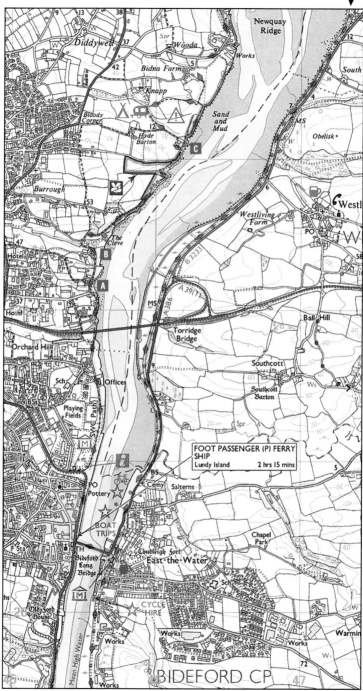

BIDEFORD

FOOT PASSENGER (P) FERRY
SHIP
Lundy Island   2 hrs 15 mins

8 km or 5 miles   Contours are given in metres
A386 Great Torrington   The vertical interval is 10m

85

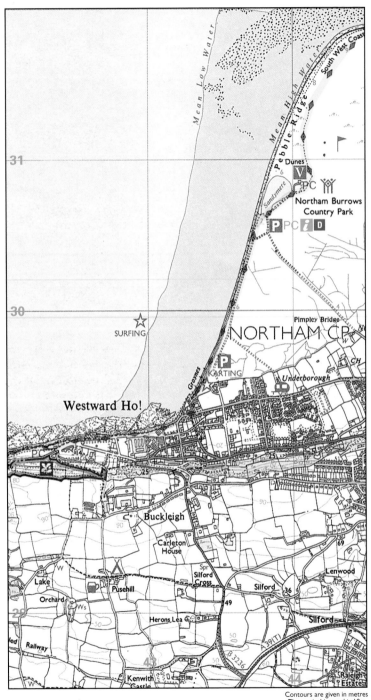

SURFING

Westward Ho!

NORTHAM C.P.

Pimpley Bridge

Dunes

Northam Burrows
Country Park

Pebble Ridge

South West Coast

Mean Low Water

Mean High Water

Sandymere

Groynes

KARTING

Underborough

CH

Buckleigh

Carleton
House

Lake

Orchard

Pusehill

Silford
Cross

Silford

Silford

Lenwood

Herons Lea

Kenwith
Castle

Raleigh
Estate

Railway

Contours are given in metres
The vertical interval is 10m

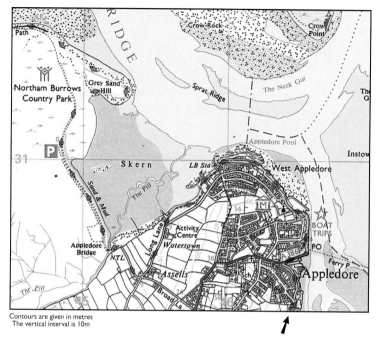

Contours are given in metres
The vertical interval is 10m

To continue towards Northam Burrows follow the riverside road (Hubbastone Road) until you come to a T-junction. Turn right towards the river, which you now follow around West Appledore. After the lifeboat station the path along the low clifftop has washed away. At low tide just keep to the beach (where you can see traces of the old coast road) as far as the Country Park past a disused boat-building hangar at Watertown. If high tide forces you to use the road turn along the road signposted for Northam Burrows Country Park. You make for the dunes ahead of you and, to your right, look across the estuary and Bideford Bar. You are now just 900 yards (825 metres) across the water from the dunes at Braunton Burrows.

The Coast Path now keeps close to the beach until it comes to the information centre **D** (10 a.m. to 5 p.m.) where there are toilets and a water tap. Keep just to the landward side of Sandymere and then along the back of the pebble ridge to Westward Ho!

Maritime enterprise in the Bristol Channel

Under Queen Elizabeth I, naval and trading activities were raised to an all-time height. At Minehead and Boscastle, old piers were given a new lease of life and at Buck's Mills, Clovelly and Hartland Quay, completely new harbours were created by the construction of piers, at enormous expense to the lords of the manors concerned. Hartland Quay, the remains of which you may see later in this walk, gained Parliamentary approval in the latter half of the 16th century and was certainly in full action by the beginning of the 17th.

The owner of Clovelly Court, George Cary, built the pier at Clovelly shortly before the end of the 16th century. The first reference to this pier is in 1597 when a labourer was paid 7d for bringing lime from Clovelly Quay to Stoke for use in the construction of the church.

These smaller quays were used mainly for local products being shipped in small quantities either from harbours on the Welsh coast or from neighbouring harbours, such as Bristol, Gloucester, Bideford and Barnstaple.

For example, in the middle of the last century, a small boat called the *Susanna* went from Hartland to Swansea and Newport to load coal, and made six trips to Caldy, Lydstep and Aberthaw to load limestone. It then went to Portgaverne, to fetch slate for building work from Delabole Quarries, while trips were also made to Barnstaple and Gloucester, quite possibly carrying farm produce from around Hartland. Occasionally, such a small boat would make a trip round Land's End in the spring if the weather was calm. Records exist to show that a later autumn trip was often made from Bideford to fetch manure to fertilise the fields, and then during the winter the ship would be laid up.

Trade from the much more important ports in the Taw and Torridge Estuaries extended much further afield, certainly to all other parts of the British Isles and to the Mediterranean and, during some periods of colonial history, as far away as America. The scene on the quaysides would have been very much more lively than it is today.

Shipbuilding and communications

Many of the small villages along this coast used to have their own shipbuilding yards. The export of tin, slate, fish, agricultural products and even some manufactured products from the hinterland all called for the supply of good strong boats.

Remember that road transport for heavy loads was slow, difficult and expensive until quite recently. Before that, sea transport reigned supreme in terms of efficiency and speed. Good access to sea transport meant easy access to the world's markets, and this is where it all happened. The first shock for the fleet operators of the ports of North Devon and Cornwall, warning of a far-reaching change in the economic life of the South West, was the coming of the railways.

Not very many years ago, Barnstaple was a major junction for railways from Ilfracombe, Bideford, Exeter and Taunton. Barnstaple Junction Station used to stand where the DIY centre is now and, although the current Barnstaple Junction Station does have a two-hourly service from Exeter, this is only a shadow of the days of the great railway era. However, the Barnstaple to Exeter line is being promoted as the scenic 'Tarka Line', a tourist route to the north coast.

The new North Devon link road, from the M5 to Barnstaple and on to Bideford, is designed to have a major effect on the economy of the area in the years to come.

Sustainable tourism

Now that much of the older industry has moved away from the area the ideal opportunity has arisen for quiet holidays in a healthy environment for which there is increasing demand in an ever more stressful world. Industrial archaeology combined with superb and colourful wildlife and landscape and fascinating geology all combine to form a sound basis for sustainable tourism as a substantial employer and money generator.

Walking, cycling, surfing, and other outdoor non-polluting sports can be combined with efficient public transport to attract visitors in an environmentally sensitive way. Some accommodation providers are catering for a profitable market in providing local organic produce combined with an emphasis on good care for the environment. Many of our visitors are enquiring about this type of facility before they decide on their holiday location. Traffic-free villages in other countries are attracting an ever increasing share of this lucrative trade. Projects like the Hartland & North Cornwall Heritage Coasts, the Exmoor National Park and the Tarka Trail are helping the South West to attract visitors who are keen to protect the environment we have all come to enjoy.

Ilfracombe Harbour and Lantern Hill.

7 Westward Ho! to Clovelly

along The Hobby Drive
11 miles (17.9 km)

As you pass the last of the chalets going west of Westward Ho! you follow a coastal track which was the old Westward Ho!–Bideford railway. Keep to this until it branches inland at Cornborough Cliff and then go along the back of the beach rise over Abbotsham Cliff, drop down, then rise again over Green Cliff **22**. A seam of anthracite was exploited here in 1805 and used to fire the nearby lime kilns.

The Coast Path continues due south-west, running into a wild hummocky area above some rather dramatic folding formations on the beach below, and then zigzags up to the summit of the cliff where it strikes south-west again, looking directly towards Buck's Mills, with Clovelly further along.

Westward Ho!, where Rudyard Kipling went to school, viewed from Northam Burrows Pebble Ridge.

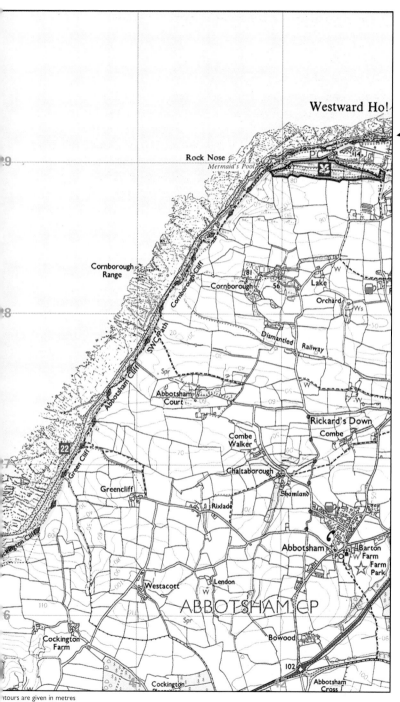

Westward Ho!

Rock Nose
Mermaid's Pool

Cornborough
Range

Cornborough Cliff

Cornborough

56

Lake

Orchard

81

Ws

W

Dismantled Railway

SWC Path

Spr

Abbotsham
Court

Abbotsham Cliff

Rickard's Down

Combe

Combe
Walker

Green Cliff

22

Chaltaborough

Greencliff

Shamland

ckington Cliff

Rixlade

Abbotsham

Barton
Farm

Farm
Park

PO

Westacott

Lendon

W

ABBOTSHAM CP

Spr

110

Cockington
Farm

Bowood

102

Cockington
Pl

Abbotsham
Cross

ntours are given in metres
e vertical interval is 10m

93

The path now crosses a substantial Devon field boundary to continue south-west along the cliff top, then begins to drop steeply into the combe just north of Westacott Cliff, descending a series of steps at the mouth of the stream **A**. Here it crosses the pebble beach for 15–20 yards before zigzagging back towards the top of the cliff via a wooden staircase.

Follow the top of Westacott Cliff and dip down to another stream before passing through a delightful thicket of willow, hawthorn and hazel, where the speckled wood butterfly is in residence. A carpet of woodland flowers clothes the ground. You emerge from this on to Higher Rowden, where the path follows the clifftop slopes just outside the field fence. Pass the track that comes down from Portledge and cross the stream in the hollow by the footbridge, continuing along the cliff top all the way to Peppercombe, where the path branches briefly inland across the combe to climb back towards the sea. Little evidence remains of the earthwork at Peppercombe Castle.

Carry on through Sloo Wood and enter Worthygate Wood. The path drops steeply to Buck's Mills, passing just to the landward side of the old coastguard lookout and arriving at the village street above the beach and next to the telephone kiosk. A quick visit to the rocky beach is worthwhile. The steep incline was built to take loads of lime brought across from the Welsh coast opposite and processed in the lime kilns, one of which is buttressed and so substantial that it could be mistaken for a ruined castle. The boats were, and still are, landed and launched straight from the beach.

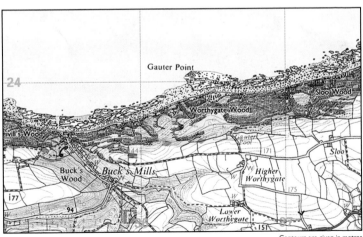

Contours are given in metres
The vertical interval is 5m

There is a small shop here which sells teas, coffees, ice creams and hot pasties. From the seaward side of the shop, take a small pathway west, which has stone steps. This rises into Buck's Wood, part of a nature reserve, where a narrow track zigzags up the side of the valley and then turns right towards the cliffs to emerge into a more open area with newly planted trees.

Contours are given in metres
The vertical interval is 5m

Continue along the clifftop path in some more woodland, keeping due west below Walland Cary, an old stately home that is now a holiday centre. Walland Cary inherited its name from Henry de la Wallen, lord of the manor in the reign of Edward I in the late 13th century.

The path is well marked as it winds up and down through this wild and ancient wood, keeping parallel to the sea. Then it rises and goes inland to emerge in to the clifftop fields over a wooden stile. Turn right and keep going along the seaward edge of the field as far as a stile leading into the woods. The path keeps just inside the wood going seawards once again, stays inside the wood going west, and then emerges into fields again. At the far western side of the second field, turn inland for another hundred yards or so and you will see another stile which takes you down to a bridge over a small stream. The path climbs steeply out of the ravine and you turn right onto The Hobby Drive.

Turn westwards and follow this drive for the next 2–3 miles (3–4 km). The occasional car may pass as this is a toll road and alternative route to Clovelly.

The Hobby Drive was built in the early 19th century under the direction of the owner, Sir James Hamlyn Williams. Such projects were often started to occupy Napoleonic prisoners of

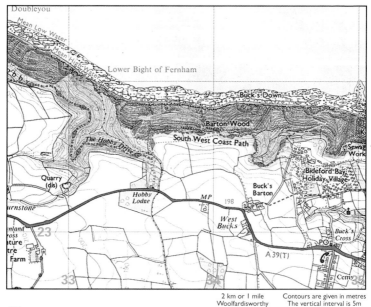

2 km or 1 mile
Woolfardisworthy

Contours are given in metres
The vertical interval is 5m

Clovelly, where the young Charles Kingsley's father was rector, seen from The Hobby Drive.

war, or to provide employment during times of economic depression.

Allow at least one hour for this walk because you must follow The Drive inland twice, quite a long way, before you reach the harbour at Clovelly.

(If you are coming from the west, you find The Hobby Drive by entering the woods next to a small monument at Mount Pleasant (NT) at the top of a cobbled track that leads up from the main street of Clovelly. Then keep on along The Hobby Drive, crossing four stone bridges. After the fourth bridge, keep eastwards along The Drive and, just as it turns northwards, you will see a small path descending to a stream to the east. Follow this path over the bridge, emerge into the field, go a hundred yards seawards, and then keep parallel to Barton Wood until you see a stile into it. Keep along the edge of the woods, just inside them, until you emerge into a large open field where you turn eastwards, remaining close to the woods, until you see a stile which takes you into a small overgrown area. Go down towards the sea briefly and then through the woods on a well-marked path due east until you reach the path that brings you to Buck's Wood and Buck's Mills. From Buck's Mills look for the telephone box, follow the small track above in a south-easterly direction and keep along the top of the clifftop slopes just inside Worthygate Woods.)

In spite of its reputation as a tourist trap, there is no escaping the fact that Clovelly is unique. Therefore, although the Coast Path continues well above the village, I heartily recommend a short-cut signed down to the village just before the western end of The Hobby Drive, visiting the harbour and then ascending the steep cobbled village street. There are pubs, tea houses and a number of places that offer bed and breakfast.

One family, the Careys of Clovelly, owned this area for four hundred years from the 14th to the 18th century, building and maintaining the famous stone pier that made a safe haven for the local fishing boats to set out to sea for shoals of herring. In 1730 the estate was sold to Zachary Hamlyn whose descendants have managed it since.

The church at Clovelly is also worth a visit. It has a Jacobean pulpit and a memorial to Charles Kingsley. The Reverend Charles Kingsley Senior came here as parish priest when his son was about 11. Apparently, the older Kingsley was a good sailor and skilful fisherman, and when the fishing fleet went to sea he would descend to the quay to conduct a parting service.

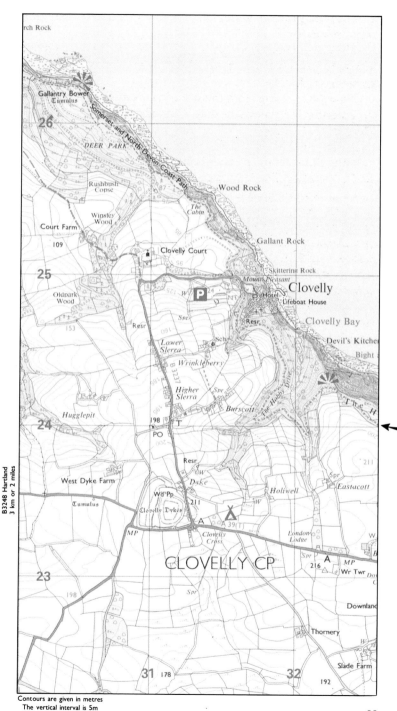

rch Rock

Gallantry Bower
Tumulus

26

DEER PARK

Rushbush
Copse

Wood Rock

Winsley
Wood

The
Cabin

Court Farm

109

Clovelly Court

Gallant Rock

Skittering Rock

25

Oldpark
Wood

Mount Pleasant

P

NT

Clovelly

Hotel

Lifeboat House

Clovelly Bay

153

Resr

Spr

Resr

Devil's Kitchen

Lower
Slerra

Sch

Bight

Wrinkleberry

Higher
Slerra

Spr

Hugglepit

Burscott

The H

24

198

T

PO

Resr

Dyke

211

West Dyke Farm

Wd Pp

Holiwell

Eastacott

Tumulus

Clovelly Dykes

211

Spr

39(T)

London
Lodge

MP

Clovelly
Cross

A

MP

B

23

CLOVELLY CP

216

Wr Twr

198

Spr

Downland

Thornery

31

178

32

Slade Farm

192

Contours are given in metres
The vertical interval is 5m

B3248 Hartland
3 km or 2 miles

99

Marine wildlife found on the North Devon and Cornwall coasts

Coastal walking offers a unique opportunity to explore both terrestrial and marine wildlife. It is well worth taking the time to look seawards and consider the wealth of life beneath the waves. Walking with an aqualung in your rucksack might be a little impractical, but the large tidal range that is a feature of this coast gives plenty of scope for exploring the seashores. Where the path plunges down to sea level, take a breather and see what you can find in the rock pools.

The marine inhabitants of this stretch of coast certainly do not have an easy life. They must withstand the full force of an Atlantic swell and the drying effects of wind and sun. The small white barnacles that encrust the rocks thrive on wave action. They are close relatives of shrimps and prawns and, although they are cemented to the rocks, they filter food from the passing water with their legs. The blue-black mussels, however, prefer a more sheltered home and can often be found in crevices on the landward side of the rocks and boulders. Round, flat limpet shells are a familiar sight and are an ideal shape for hanging on to the rock. They graze algae from the rock surface and always return 'home', where they fit the rock perfectly.

These, and other shellfish, often fall prey to the dog whelk, which drills a hole through the shell and sucks out the unfortunate victim! Dog whelk eggs, like rows of small yellow milk bottles on the undersides of the rocks, are also a common sight. The beadlet anemone, like a blob of jelly, withdraws its stinging tentacles while the tide is out. All three colour forms of this anemone – green, red and 'strawberry' – occur along this coast.

Seaweeds, high up on the shore, tend to be stunted by the pounding waves. In rock pools, however, they make a colourful garden. The pink, encrusting weed and the coarse, tufted coralline weed contrast with the bright green and brown weeds. If you are fortunate enough to visit one of the many rocky shores at a very low tide, you will glimpse the kelp forest below low-water mark. Among these huge, strap-like seaweeds, urchins, starfish, sea-slugs, sponges, crabs and lobsters make their homes. Pollock, wrasse, conger and bass shelter among the kelp. These provide food for sea birds, such as puffins, gannets and cormorants, and for the grey seals that breed in the caves and bays of Hartland and Lundy.

This coast is fed by the Gulf Stream and therefore can boast several marine creatures that are not found on other parts of the English coast. The snakelocks anemone, with its long, wavy tentacles, is a common sight in rock pools but the dahlia anemone, with its striped tentacles and sticky column, covered with shell fragments, is a rare find.

Rocks and rock pools often occur alongside sandy shores, which appear barren in comparison. The sand is constantly scoured by the waves, so its inhabitants live safely buried beneath the surface. Shells cast up on the shore give an idea of what lives below. A walk after a storm can reveal some fascinating finds: egg cases of skate or dogfish (mermaid's purses), cuttlefish bones and goose barnacles covering plastic containers.

The estuaries at either end of this path support a wealth of fascinating wildlife, influenced by fresh and salt water. The mudflats, exposed at low tide, and the saltmarsh areas support many plants, shellfish and worms, which in turn provide food for birds. The Taw and Torridge Estuaries are of national and regional importance for wintering wildfowl and waders: wigeon, shelduck, oystercatcher, golden and ringed plover, redshank and curlew, to mention just a few. In the sheltered upper-shore regions of the estuaries, periwinkles and seaweeds such as bladder wrack and egg wrack, more familiar on rocky beaches, cling to pebbles and empty shells surprisingly far upriver. The balance of life is delicate in this estuarine community and is therefore highly vulnerable to pollution.

Another interesting feature of the estuaries are the sand dunes, found on the seaward margins. Coarse marram grass binds the sand together on the newer dunes. The intermediate ridges are colonised by other plants until they become grass-covered and grazed by rabbits. In the damp slacks between the ridges grow scrub plants, such as blackthorn, and this is an excellent place for wild flowers and insects. The Braunton Burrows area is a nature reserve of international repute. Some plants such as the tiny French toadflax grow nowhere else in Britain.

It is an exciting time for coastal management. The lessons learned through pioneering work on the Heritage Coasts are now being applied on a wider scale. Management is being achieved by cooperation between coastal interests through voluntary groups, and coastal managers are being encouraged to 'look out to the sea' and consider the *whole* coast as an ecologically integrated entity.

8 Clovelly to Hartland Quay

passing Gallantry Bower and Windbury Waterfall
9¾ miles (15.7 km)

Going westwards from Clovelly is not quite as straightforward as it looks on many maps. If you are emerging from The Hobby Drive where the steep, small track from the village meets the road, go north along the road for a short distance. The road then turns inland and a very narrow, steep track leads seawards **A**. Go through the wooden gate into the field at this fork and skirt round the seaward side of the field. At the far end go through the metal kissing gate into the next field. Keep close to the woods until you come to another kissing gate that takes you into a long, dark, rhododendron tunnel, emerging at 'The Cabin'.

For the next half-mile (800 metres), the path keeps in a general north-westerly direction, parallel to the steeply sloping top of the cliff. The route runs through woodland and takes you past several intriguing shelters. Just before descending to Mouth Mill there is a short detour through the woods to another of these whimsical structures.

Clovelly's pier, built to the orders of one Charles Carey, lawyer, in the 16th century, used to shelter a fleet of 60 fishing boats.

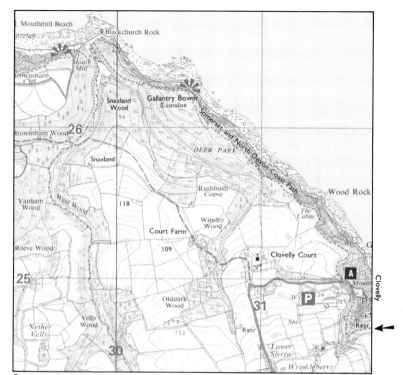

Contours are given in metres
The vertical interval is 5m

From here to Hartland Point is about 5 miles (8 km) and, apart from places where the path zigzags to cross steep valleys, you travel more or less due west and on the cliff top all the way.

From Gallantry Bower (325 feet/100 metres in height), the path first clings to the cliff top, down a steep, overgrown slope. As it enters more mature woodland it zigzags down to a forest track which leads to Mouthmill Beach and its lime kiln. On the rocky beach is Blackchurch Rock, with its two natural archways.

(If you are going eastwards towards Clovelly, follow the track on the eastern side of the stream, which rises up through the woodland, and at the top of the forestry track you will see a path zigzagging coastwards. Within a few yards you will come to the cliff top which you follow all the way to Clovelly.)

If you are continuing westwards, go to the western side of the stream and the small track inland, past buildings that were once a tea house. Find a path climbing right through the woods, emerging at the top of a very steep slope into a field with superb views of Blackchurch Rock and the North Devon coast.

103

Keep to the seaward side of the fields, parallel to the sea, until you come to a stile on National Trust property leading to the steep zigzag path down to Windbury Waterfall **B**. At the bottom of this valley, and very close to the sea and cliff top, cross the wooden footbridge. On the western side of this a track leads upstream and inland for about a hundred yards before the Coast Path returns northwards to the cliff top. There it turns westwards to reach Windbury Head at 468 feet (135 metres) and its prehistoric earthwork. The prominent red outcrop is Exmansworthy Cliff. The National Trust has recently signed paths connecting the Coast Path with their car park at Exmansworthy Farm just inland.

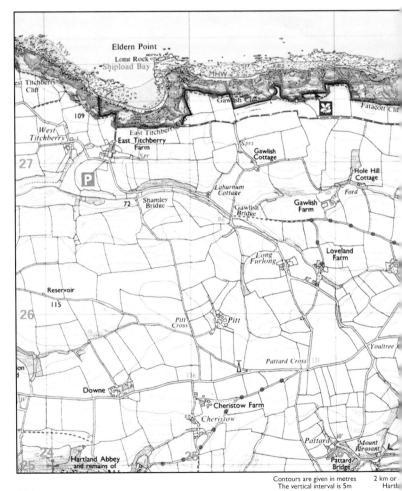

Contours are given in metres
The vertical interval is 5m

There are no major climbs or descents from here until you reach Hartland Point, approximately 4 miles (6.4 km) away.

Keep just inside the fields at the top of Fatacott Cliff until you come to a National Trust sign for Gawlish, from where the Coast Path winds its way past some small terraced fields to a stile. Just to the east of Shipload Bay the path stays outside the fence, clinging to the top of East Titchberry Cliff. Here it meets a bridleway running east–west, which you follow past a small path leading to Shipload Bay (closed as at 1998 because of landslips).

There is a sharp bend in the bridleway taking it south to East Titchberry, and at this point the Coast Path turns a few yards seawards before entering the fields and keeping to the cliff top.

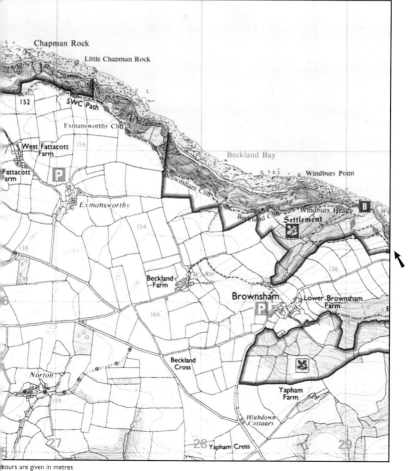

tours are given in metres
e vertical interval is 5m

Just to the east of Hartland Point **23** the Coast Path is outside the fence. After passing to the seaward side of the radar tower you will see a small car park with a tea kiosk, open at Easter and then from May to September.

(Those who have arrived from the west should keep along the cliff, setting off in a north-easterly direction. They should then keep more or less on the immediate cliff top to Windbury Waterfall **B**.)

To continue west, leave the car park by the Lighthouse Road past a notice saying 'No Unauthorised Vehicles'. Note the water collection system: a large area of concrete that feeds into a tank on the opposite side of the road. It used to supply water to the lighthouse. Also note the Trinity House property way-mark boundary. Just past a small, square, flat-roofed store-room, the Coast Path turns west up a steep concrete path with some steps and a wicket gate, and then makes for the tall square of security barbed-wire fencing surrounding a coast-guard lookout, now manned only on an occasional basis. The Coast Path continues south-west, down from the headland, and follows the cliffs.

Suddenly, a view southwards opens up, with Damehole Point and Gull Rock standing out prominently across two small coves, and a strange, lonely, wild little valley behind, called Smoothlands. The Coast Path runs along Upright Cliff and then descends steeply to Titchberry Water, where there is a path down to the beach.

Make your way upstream to the footbridge across Titchberry Water, with a stile on each side, then climb a flight of wooden steps. At the top of the steep slope the Coast Path goes over a stile and seawards, parallel with the stream below, with a high hedgewall on the southern side. Going south and west now the path leaves the edge of the field and descends into Smooth-lands. It keeps along the bottom of this old hanging valley, which evidently was once the bed of the stream that now runs into the cove to the north. The valley floor is covered in gorse and bracken with small outcrops of heather and stonecrop and some giant ant hills.

Soon you come to a number of stepping stones over a marshy spot, beyond which is a small rocky cove. This is Damehole Point, halfway between Hartland Point and Hartland Quay. Go up the slope on the southern side of Smoothlands valley and you will see Stoke Church tower **24** and also a tower that stands behind Hartland Quay. Beware of the holes near the edge of

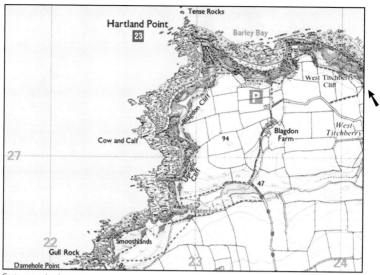

Contours are given in metres
The vertical interval is 5m

Rock strata etched out by the Atlantic waves below Upright Cliff. The complex geology here is best studied from the Coast Path.

the cliff where there is serious subsidence. This is Blegberry Cliff and the Coast Path stays close to it, dropping steeply down into Blegberry Water, with its waterfall, before rising steeply to the top of a sheer slab of rock 650 feet (200 metres) above the sea.

Stoke Church **24** can be seen once again at the head of the valley which contains Hartland Abbey. Descend into the valley, go behind the cottage just back from the beach, and cross a small bridge to the east of it. The cottage was Blackpool Mill and the river is called the Abbey River. Go through an iron kissing gate just behind the cottages, and upstream for about a hundred yards to cross the bridge. Then turn back immediately towards the coast and climb due south just inland of Dyer's Lookout.

Continuing south and west you soon come to the top of Warren Cliff and within sight of Hartland Quay **25**.

Keep back from the cliff top, go just in front of the rocket apparatus house, and take a track and then the small road leading down to the quay.

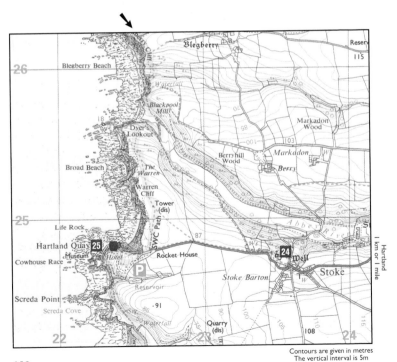

Contours are given in metres
The vertical interval is 5m

Hartland Quay from Damehole Point. Visit the museum at Hartland Quay for a fascinating picture of this area's past.

The history of Hartland Quay

There was a harbour at Hartland Quay until the end of the last century, when the railway reached Bideford and road transport improved, so it became uneconomic to repair storm damage and keep up the quay. If you have walked this section of coast during stormy weather you will be amazed that any man-made structure managed to survive the 300 years that it did. It is supposed that the massive rocks used for its foundations were roped to sealed empty barrels, moved into position at high tide and the ropes cut in the appropriate place to bed the stone in.

During the 17th century the property passed to the Luttrells of Dunster and it is assumed that at this time the Merchants House and stores, which still stand, and the lime kiln at the quay were built.

In the middle of the 19th century Hartland Quay supported two families of working men, a servant, a coastguard, a publican and possibly a maltster. A visit to the Hartland Quay Museum is recommended.

9 Hartland Quay to Bude

via Higher Sharpnose Point
15 miles (24.1 km)

To continue south, retrace your steps up the hill and then go through a kissing gate. A few hundred yards to the south of Hartland Quay you will see Screda Point with its sheer, jagged plates of slate thrusting out of the sea.

The Coast Path skirts round the landward side of St Catherine's Tor and crosses a stream on some round concrete stepping stones. The former dam behind the high stone boundary was the swan pool for Hartland Abbey. Make for a wicket gate in the wall opposite. Having gone through the wicket gate, turn seawards along the wall for about 20 yards and then strike south at a 45-degree angle up the slope, to emerge on the cliff top where it overlooks yet another rocky bay. Rise again to 200 feet (60 metres) round the back of this bay and cross the field boundary stile.

The stony path becomes narrower and steeper, and drops on a zigzag down to the flat area around the dramatic waterfalls at Speke's Mill Mouth. The meadow through which you pass is covered in eyebright, yarrow and wood sage, with little clumps of heather and milkwort. If it has been dry you can cross the stream on a ridge of rock a few yards above the waterfall. Otherwise, go upstream for 300 yards (275 metres) and cross the footbridge. Keep straight ahead, south-west, across the valley or climb a valley that runs up the landward side of Swansford Hill and then leave the valley and follow the cliff top for the next mile (1.6 km).

The Coast Path comes to a ditch where you have to go inland for a few yards to cross it. For the youth hostel **26**, strike inland on the northern side of this ditch through a gateway with a stile, then keep straight inland and you come to the phone box at Elmscott. Turn right (south) and you reach the youth hostel.

If you are continuing, keep south along the clifftop path until you see a sunken triangular field on your right (west). At this point keep to the field boundary and make for the stile in the corner, which brings you out on a country lane. Turn right (south-west) and continue down this lane for 700 yards (640 metres) before turning right (west) down a field track, keeping to the northern side of a substantial field boundary, until you come to the cliffs.

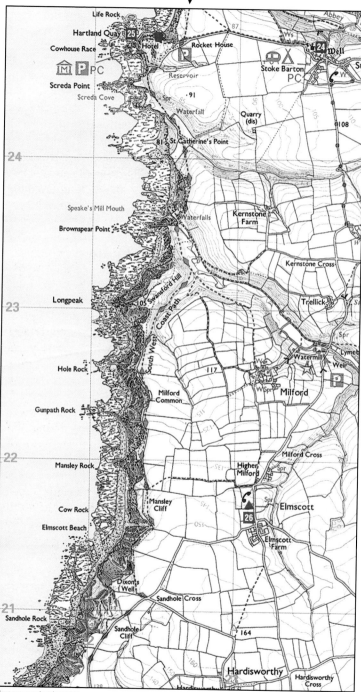

Contours are given in metres
The vertical interval is 5m

Basically, the Coast Path now follows the cliff top the whole way to Bude, rising frequently to about 500 feet (150 metres), then dipping to sea level, only to rise again on the other side of the valley. You should be a good deal fitter when you get to the other end! Going south you will see the buildings of South Hole 300 yards (275 metres) inland.

Pass the track which leads down to South Hole and climb to the Iron Age ramparts at the hill fort of Embury Beacon **27**(515 feet/157 metres). The promontory forts at Hillsborough, just to the east of Ilfracombe, the most distinct example on this path, and the defensive earthworks above Sillery, between Countisbury and Lynton, would be of a similar age. Elsewhere along the path there is evidence of two other main periods of premedieval occupation. The many small mounds can be assumed to be evidence of a Bronze Age civilisation, and the standing stones near the Coast Path, particularly between Lee and Mortehoe, were probably erected during the same period. You may also remember the Roman fortlet at Martinhoe, where excavation showed the remains of the barrack buildings, with field ovens at the back of the earth ramparts, an armourers' furnace and evidence of the signal fires on the cliff top. At Tintagel Church there are Roman boundary markers referred to locally as milestones.

Half a mile (1 km) south of Embury, the path passes Knap Head before coming to the steep slope down into Welcombe Mouth, where there is a small car park and some sand on the beach. Cross the stream by the round stepping stones and leave on the track from the seaward end of the car park. You now climb to 400 feet (122 metres) and are soon overlooking Marsland Mouth, which, with its wooded valley, is a reserve managed jointly by the Devon and Cornwall Wildlife Trusts. You can see quite clearly how the path emerges from the southern side of the valley in a wide zigzag sweep. As you cross the footbridge over the stream you enter Cornwall. Note the mill wheel on West Mill **28** just upstream. Rise again to 400 feet (122 metres) at Marsland Cliff.

The next steep valley to negotiate is Litter Mouth, where the Coast Path descends on wooden steps and rises at a safe distance from the cliff top. Follow the cliff top to Yeolmouth Cliff and look back north at Gull Rock **29**, which has a square hole through it called Devil's Hole. Then there is another dip towards Yeolmouth and a rise to Henna Cliff. If you come down from Henna Cliff into Morwenstow look carefully at the

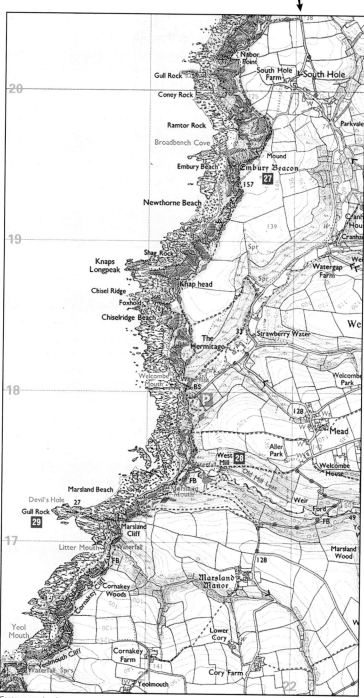

Contours are given in metres
The vertical interval is 5m

vicarage building to the left of the church **30**. The eccentric Parson Hawker who came here as vicar in 1834 replaced the derelict vicarage with a mock Gothic structure adding his own mark with strange chimneys. He is credited with starting the Harvest Festival service and wrote the Cornish anthem 'Shall Trelawney Die'.

As you scramble down into the deep valley where the map shows St Morwenna's Well and a waterfall (neither of which is visible from the Coast Path), you will see a fine selection of plants characteristic of the area: heather, scabious, sea carrot, kidney vetch, birdsfoot trefoil, sea campion and stonecrop. Here, while the Coast Path is still within sight of the tower of Morwenstow, a path from the village joins it.

Just to the south of this you will come to a National Trust sign saying 'Hawker's hut' **31**. Go down a few steps and you willsee a wooden-doored, wooden-walled, wooden-seated, turf-covered hut nestling under sea-thrift and stonecrop and giving a magnificent view out to sea. Hawker was the vicar of Morwenstow for 40 years. He used driftwood to build his hut and, wearing a fisherman's jumper of the special Morwenstow knit pattern and boots, in addition to his cassock, he used it as a place of meditation, wrote some of his poetry here, and occasionally enjoyed an opium pipe.

As you approach Higher Sharpnose Point you will see a stream called The Tidna. The path zigzags steeply down to this, crosses a wooden bridge, goes over a stile, and then turns seawards to mount diagonally towards the summit of Higher Sharpnose Point **A** with some magnificent views. At the top of Higher Sharpnose Point you come to an old ruined coastguard station where the path turns back south-east along the cliff. This piece of the path is not for those who do not enjoy giddy heights.

Soon you come to Stanbury Mouth where you have to zigzag briefly inland and back to the footbridge, mount wooden steps to a stile, and continue south straight up the hill. From Stanbury Mouth there is also a path inland. The Coast Path takes you near the Composite Signals Organisation Station at Cleave Camp, where massive satellite-tracking dish aerials dominate the coastal scene. As you pass the boundary fence of this establishment, branch seawards, without dropping too much, to enjoy the views from Lower Sharpnose Point, and then keep on along the gorse-covered cliff top. Soon you come to the National Trust sign which says 'Coastal Path to Duckpool'.

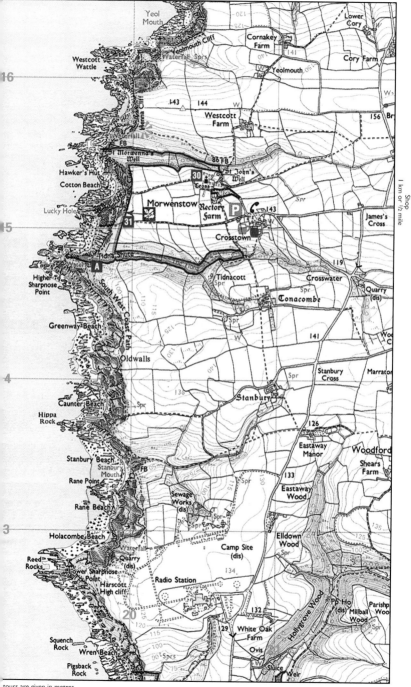

Coombe Valley. The farm at Stowe Barton (centre top) was the site of a great Restoration-period mansion.

When you reach the very steep slope overlooking the Coombe Valley, look inland and enjoy the view to Kilkhampton Church standing on the hill at the end of the valley. Nearly all the fields you can see from Steeple Point belonged to the Grenville family from the 12th to the 18th centuries. This family became famous during the Tudor and Stuart reigns, and Roger Grenville was captain of the *Mary Rose*. This galleon sank off Portsmouth in 1545, with the King looking on, and has now been raised and put on display in Portsmouth. Other members of the family played prominent roles in the army and navy during the 16th and 17th centuries. One of the last members of the family to achieve fame was John Grenville, who helped greatly in the Restoration of the Stuart monarchy. As a result he became Earl of Bath, Governor of Plymouth, and Lord Lieutenant of Cornwall and was able to build a large four-storey mansion. If you look across the valley you will see a group of farm buildings. This was the site of his house **32**, demolished only 60 years after it had been built because Sir John's sister preferred to live elsewhere.

If you look upstream towards the top of the meadow you will see a small bridge **33**. Parson Hawker took note of the locals' concern that the stream here was often difficult to ford. He started a subscription list and made a request to the King, who began the fund with a donation of £20. It is called King William's Bridge and was completed in 1836.

Going south from Duckpool the path climbs in a wide zigzag sweep to the top of Warren Point before dropping to Warren Gutter, where a stream drops down to a rocky beach where the rock formations are exposed horizontally. Continuing along the cliff top for another half mile (1 km) south, the Coast Path comes to Sandy Mouth where there is a National Trust car park, refreshments in season, and toilets.

All the way from Duckpool to Bude there are sandy beaches at low tide. Bathing can be dangerous, however, particularly at low tide when the coastal currents can be very strong. Please observe any warning notices, flags or lifeguard instructions. It is generally safer to swim on an incoming tide than an outgoing one.

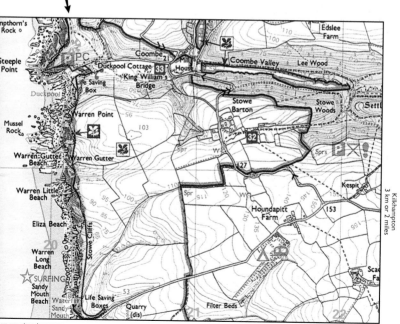

urs are given in metres
vertical interval is 5m

South of Sandy Mouth, past Menachurch Point (note the Bronze Age tumulus **34**), the Coast Path follows the cliff top to Crooklets and from there stays close to the beach along a permissive path until you come alongside the River Neet in Bude. Cross the first bridge you come to and carry straight on down the street opposite. Turn right (north-west) when you come to the second stretch of water which is the old Bude Canal. After visiting Bude Stratton Museum on the quay, walk seawards until you reach the canal lock. Cross the lock and continue to follow the cliff top towards Efford Down.

The tramway on the Canal Basin at Bude. The canal was built in 1823 to take calcium-rich beach sand from Bude to inland farms.

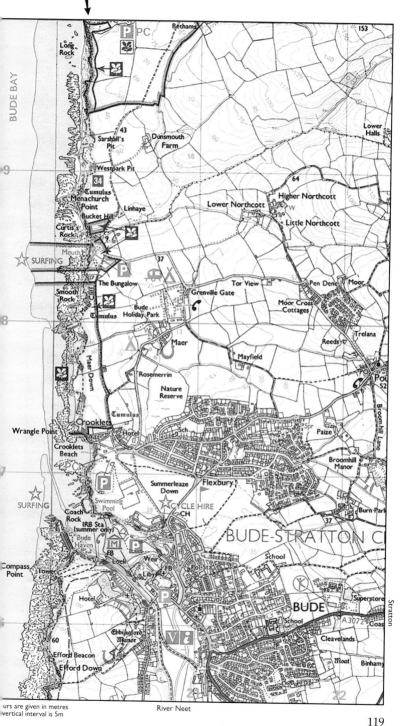

ur s are given in metres
vertical interval is 5m

River Neet

10 Bude to Boscastle Harbour

via Pencannow and Crackington Haven
16½ miles (26.5 km)

It would be difficult to get lost on the next stretch of Coast Path, to Widemouth. It hugs the cliff top and the back of the beaches all the way and runs alongside the Bude–Widemouth road for part of its length. Simply follow the low cliff top until you are just half a mile (1 km) south of Widemouth.

A CIRCULAR WALK FROM BUDE

6 miles (9.7 km)
(see map opposite)

Park in the town and cross the River Neet. Make your way alongside the canal which runs west of the river towards the sea. Note lines which are still in place from the tramway, used to transfer goods from moored sea-going boats to the canal barges. The Castle between the canal and the river was built by Sir Goldsworthy Gurney, the Cornish engineer responsible for one of the earliest steam locomotives.

Cross the lock and turn right and follow the road seawards until you see a wicket gate. Go through this onto the open clifftop and make for Compass Point, so-called because of the folly there adorned with the points of the compass. Looking up the coast to the north you may see the one-acre saltwater swimming pool, built in the late 1800s after the railway started bringing ever larger numbers of visitors, and still well used.

Keep on along the cliffs until you come to Lower Longbeak, overlooking Widemouth Sand. There is a car park here to give access to the headland. Just north of the salt house, which is the first house to come between the cliffs and the coast path after leaving Bude, make for the road and a stile and gate giving access to a path across the fields. Go north east to the top corner of the field and straight ahead for the far side of the next field. Follow the next field boundary, and then head north-east again to join a drive leading to a bridge over a stream. Just before the bridge turn left along a permissive path and join the canal tow path. Follow this back into Bude.

You could also start this walk from Lower Longbeak car park just north of Widemouth. There are information points along the path which explain the history of the canal.

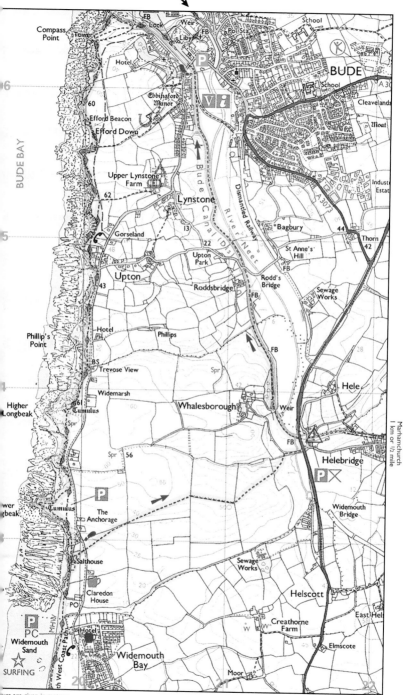

BUDE BAY

Compass
Point
Tower

FB
Lock
Weir
Libry
FB
Po. St.
School

P

Hotel

V i

BUDE

School

A 30

Cleavelands

Moat

60

Ebbingford
Manor

Efford Beacon

Efford Down

Upper Lynstone
Farm

62

Lynstone

13

Gorseland

22

Upton
Park

Upton

43

Roddsbridge

FB

Bude Canal (Dis)

River Neet

Dismantled Railway

A 303

Bagbury

St Anne's
Hill

FB

Rodd's
Bridge

Sewage
Works

44

Thorn
42

Phillip's
Point

Hotel

Phillips

BS

Trevose View

FB

28

Hele

Higher
Longbeak

Widemarsh

Tumulus

Spr

Whalesborough

Weir

FB

Helebridge

P X

wer
gbeak

Tumulus

P

The
Anchorage

Spr 56

Widemouth
Bridge

Salthouse

Sewage
Works

Claredon
House

PO

Helscott

East Hel

P
PC

MHW

Hotel

Creathorne
Farm

Elmscote

Widemouth
Sand

SURFING

South West Coast Path

Widemouth
Bay

Moor

20

22

Marhamchurch
I km or ½ mile

urs are given in metres
vertical interval is 5m

121

You are now approaching Wanson Mouth where the cliffs have crumbled, necessitating a detour inland **A** along a track that joins the coast road. Follow the coast road, which has been reconstructed to avoid the landslips, for half a mile (1 km) south-west. At this point **B** the road turns inland and the Coast Path stays on the cliff top at Bridwill Point, turning south and away from the cliffs only on the steep descent into Millook. Join the road again at Millook to go west up the steep bit, glancing back to note the extraordinary chevron folding of the cliffs here. Keep to the cliffs where the road turns inland 300 yards (275 metres) up the hill at Raven's Beak. The Coast Path now stays on the cliff top passing above Dizzard Wood with its dwarf oaks and nationally important lichens and wild service trees, all the way to Crackington Haven, with one 250-foot (75-metre) fall and rise just south of Chipman Point.

Between Castle Point, just north of Crackington Haven, and Trebarwith Strand there are several places where it is extremely dangerous to stray from the path. Large, slippery slabs of shale or steep screes end either in rough seas or at precipice tops, and there is sometimes no way out of these areas once entered. For safe walking, caution is therefore advised. Always follow signs

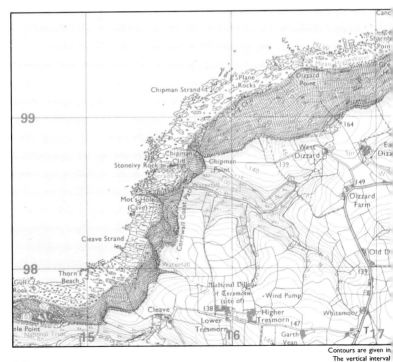

Contours are given in
The vertical interval

Black Rock

Wanson Mouth

A

Hotel

Hotel

Saltstone

Saltstone Strand

Great Wanson

67

Foxhole Point

P

Penhalt Cliff

B

Foxhole Strand

Millook Haven

Bridwill Point

Lower Penhalt

97

Raven's Beak

Gull Rock

Broad Strand

Higher Penhalt

01

00

Millook

Mill Farm

Trevisick

52

FB

Weir

Ford

18

Ford

111

Millook Common

Tumulus

Settlement

Trebarfoote Wood

Trevoulter

91

Cancleave

Level (dis)

FB

Trebarfoote

99

119

Silverdown

69

Tamp's Wood

113

The Den

Atlantic View

Landy Wood

Trengayor Copse

Lower Tregole

122

98

ayor

Tregole

Lower Trewint

133

Higher Tregole

Edelweiss

Bastard Mill

148

Middle Trewint

18

Higher Trewint

19

Meads

urs are given in metres
vertical interval is 5m

and, if in doubt, take the highest route, keeping away from the cliff edge.

At Castle Point keep to the cliff top ridge **C** and then zigzag back down to the stream at Aller Shoot. Then up the zigzag path on the headland at Pencannow and descend to Crackington Haven.

From Crackington Haven, follow the clifftop path to the south of the beach for half a mile (1 km), when you will be close to Cambeak. Here **D** make absolutely sure that you stay on the cliff top. There is a path marked going lower but this has fallen away and is dangerous. Turn south to continue, it will be helpful if you follow the permissive path above the small valley behind Cambeak which will help to reduce erosion on this much-trampled headland. When you come once more to the cliff top you should continue along it for a further half-mile (800 metres).

Just south of The Strangles, near Trevigue Farm, the Coast Path crosses a hummocky area and then goes round the back of a small valley before rising to High Cliff at over 700 feet (210 metres). To the south of High Cliff, the path descends steeply on the cliff edge until it meets a small stream which runs on the far side of a wall. Rather than attempting to cross the stream here, you should follow it seawards for about 20 yards, where you will find a footbridge that provides an easy crossing point **E**.

The next section can be dangerous if you get too low and near any screes or slate slabs. If you do, you have taken a wrong turning. Whenever in doubt, keep up and away from the cliff edge. Go seawards from the footbridge **E** for 20 yards and then follow a small ridge uphill. Follow the very narrow path, keeping more or less level around the steep slope above the sea. This path soon curves round to head south, and begins to rise along the bracken-, gorse-, and heather-covered slopes, dipping briefly before a steady climb to the crest of the heather-covered slopes. *Ignore any small tracks which go off seawards* and climb steadily to the top.

From the stile at the top of Rusey Cliff, the path has been realigned to follow the field edge. Follow the waymarks to rejoin the coastal slope at Buckator.

Soon you will see Buckator, a sheer black cliff with white bands of quartz running through it, standing next to Gull Rock, one of many on this coast with the same name, with the seething gulley between. West and ahead, you will notice a series of fingers of land and, just offshore, white foam surrounding

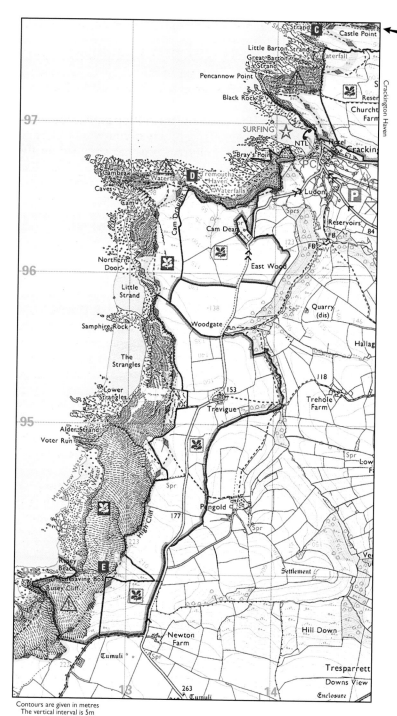

Contours are given in metres
The vertical interval is 5m

a number of rocks submerged at high tide. These are called Saddle Rock and Beeny Sisters and if you are lucky you may see seals here.

Along here the path sticks mainly to the edges of the clifftop field, occasionally venturing just outside and crossing substantial stiles to do so. Quite suddenly, at the end of a large, flat field, you will see ahead and to the south a magnificent panorama stretching from Boscastle to Tintagel, with Pentire Head and Trevose Head in the distance. The path drops abruptly down to the low Beeny Cliff.

Steps have been cut in the slate at the top and wooden steps take you on down the steepest bits westwards to Fire Beacon Point with Beeny Sisters, the seething, semi-submerged rocks, immediately below to the north. At Fire Beacon Point the Coast Path turns south, parallel with Beeny Cliff, towards the distinctive little dent called Seals Hole. Soon the path approaches Pentargon, turning gradually eastward and uphill beside some terraced fields before levelling out, still going east. Now you will come within sight of the waterfall fed by the stream from Beeny.

Wooden steps take you down to a footbridge and the Coast Path climbs steeply out of the V-shaped valley to regain its

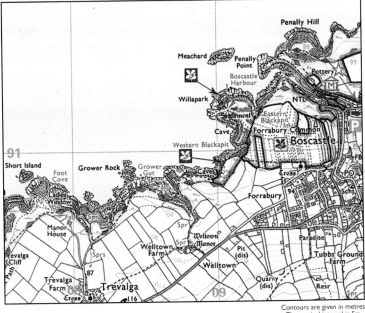

Contours are given in metres
The vertical interval is 5m

Contours are given in metres
The vertical interval is 5m

former height. Continuing from here along the cliff top on the southern side of Pentargon, the path stays on the outside of the wall at the cliff top, and crosses the corners of two fields before entering the National Trust property of Pentargon Cliff. Here it returns to being outside the wall and stays there until you are above Boscastle Harbour.

A CIRCULAR WALK FROM BOSCASTLE

4 miles (6.6 km)

Near Boscastle, a walk of 2–3 miles (3–4 km) upstream through the meadows above the car park at the Cobweb Inn brings you to the church of St Julitta **35** at Hennett, in the parish of St Juliot.

To return to Boscastle it is best initially to retrace your steps to the footbridge in Peter's Wood, which you will have passed on the way. Cross this bridge and keep on south-east through the woods until you come to Minster Church, 400 yards west of Trecarne Gate. Keep down the country lane after this, going towards the sea until you see a stile, taking the path straight ahead where the lane turns left. This path crosses the River Jordan, and brings you out at the top of Boscastle village, which is exceedingly attractive and deserves thorough exploration before you complete your circular walk at the Boscastle Harbour car park. The National Trust leaflet *Boscastle*, available at their information centre at the harbour, gives further fascinating details on the features you will see on this walk.

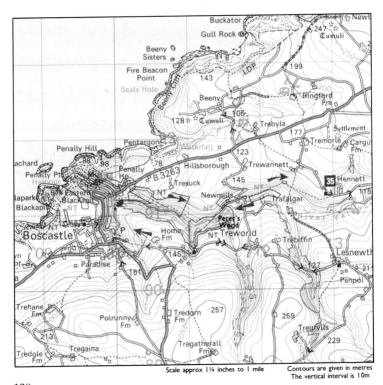

Scale approx 1¼ inches to 1 mile   Contours are given in metres
The vertical interval is 10m

Trebarwith Strand and Gull Rock at high tide.

Thomas Hardy on the Cornish coast

The Wesleyan movement in Cornwall was going from strength to strength in the latter part of the 19th century and the Anglican Church, very conscious of the competition, was keen to revitalise itself in order to counter this trend. The Dorchester firm of Hicks was commissioned to make a record of the church of St Julitta **35** with a view to its restoration, and the young Thomas Hardy, architect, who worked for Mr Hicks, came to do a survey in March 1872.

The rector's sister-in-law, Emma, was staying at the rectory at the time of Thomas Hardy's arrival. He had to make several visits and Emma, aged 29, rode her horse, while he walked alongside, to show him around the area. They would walk along the cliffs between Crackington Haven and Trebarwith, watching the surging Atlantic for seals. They walked down the Valency Valley to Boscastle and would sometimes take a horse and carriage to Tintagel, Trebarwith Strand or Bossiney.

Four years after his first arrival here, Thomas Hardy and Emma Lavinia Gifford were married, and both were later to write about their happy times on these cliffs. His novel, *A Pair of Blue Eyes*, is the story of a visit to North Cornwall by a young architect coming to restore a village church.

Boscastle Harbour

As you come down the Coast Path towards Boscastle from the north, the first group of houses on your left were the residences of the ships' captains who operated from Boscastle. These houses were constructed in the mid-19th century and you can see the sail lofts and the sailors' accommodation at the back of the courtyard. The youth hostel was the stable for the port. Opposite the youth hostel is a fisherman's house with its sail loft.

In front of the 19th century houses you can see a low range of cottages that would have been fishermen's homes with sail lofts and stores. The buildings just upstream from the Youth Hostel were probably a fish cellar of the type you can see at Portgaverne, Port Isaac and Portquin. Further up, note the lime kiln on the left. The horses would have loaded the limestone and coal shipped from South Wales from the top, using the track next to the National Trust information shop, which was the forge. If you keep left (north) past the National Trust shop you can look up a long, cobbled street, which is the original road leading down to the harbour at Boscastle. This would have been a busy scene with ship chandlers, provision shops and several pubs.

Opposite the car park, as you come up through the village, is the Cobweb Inn. This was one of the many developments which took place in Boscastle during the last century, making it a moderately important trading port, and used to be the warehouse and depot of Sloggatt and Rosevear, wine merchants. The Cobweb Inn is so called because the firm used to keep its barrels of sherry and wine on the ground floor. Cobwebs and spiders were encouraged in order to keep the number of flies down. Any employee found removing the cobwebs was liable to be dismissed.

During 1893, the North Cornwall Railway arrived at Camelford, and on Wednesday 8th October 1893 it reached the Delabole Slate Quarries. The Delabole Brass Brand was brought out, a performance was laid on by the Royal Marines Band from Plymouth, and a free lunch was given for all the villagers, railway workers and slate quarry workers in a marquee erected near the station. This was followed by sports and fireworks. From this date the ports of North Cornwall would never be the same again. The quickest and safest means of exporting local products was to be via the Railway Goods Depot at Camelford

Boscastle Harbour, a retreat from storms and pirates, and an important trading point for north Cornwall before the railway era.

Station or, in the case of the slates, directly from the quarry, a process which at Delabole stopped only in 1966 with the Beeching cuts. Fishing did continue, however, and still does, and the railway brought the first large numbers of tourists, whose expenditure helped to fill the gap caused in the local economy by the transport and economic changes.

A railway project for Boscastle never materialised. Hence, horse-drawn coaches continued to serve the village until the 1920s, at which point the petrol-engined charabanc took over. As a result, the Wellington Hotel, which changed its name from the Boscastle Hotel on the Duke's death in 1852, was one of the last staging inns in England.

Now you can find out all about Boscastle, the wildlife, geology and everything else about the North Cornwall coast at the new Visitor Centre in the car park at Boscastle, run by the North Cornwall Heritage Coast and Countryside Service.

11 Boscastle Harbour to Tintagel Haven

via the Rocky Valley and Willapark
4¾ miles (7.6 km)

Go along the southern side of the natural harbour at Boscastle, pass the quay, and beside it you will find a small rocky path. Keep well away from the cliff as it can be slippery. Stay parallel to the bend of the harbour until you can see the former Willapark coastguard station, originally built as a summer house. The Coast Path cuts straight across the headlands with ancient strip-field systems on your landward side.

The promontory-fort at Willapark is thought to have been constructed around 200 BC, but the Bronze Age tumuli (burial mounds) you can see just inland are probably more than 3,000 years old, and evidence of Stone Age occupation, including flint weapons and working tools, has been found.

The strip fields adjacent to Willapark are called, locally, 'stitches'. Most are owned by the National Trust. The farming tenants may crop their fields from Lady Day to Michaelmas (25th March – 29th September) but during the rest of the year the fields remain common land for grazing.

Continuing south and west, the cliff slate workings at Western Blackapit were called California Quarry. The National Trust leaflets *Boscastle* and *Tintagel* give detailed descriptions of how the men and boys who worked here were lowered down over the cliff to set the dynamite charges and win the slate under the most dangerous conditions.

Keep your eyes open for seals around these parts. The Coast Path keeps just to the seaward side of a substantial slate wall, crosses over a slate stile and then a wooden one, then goes down into Grower Gut, a steep little rocky valley below Welltown. You drop steeply to the stream down a set of steps and a zigzag path, cross the footbridge and then cross the stile and another small footbridge to continue westwards. A little later, if you look back across Grower Gut, you can see one of the old mining galleries cut into the cliff.

West of Grower Gut, the path goes round the edge of the field to the cliff top. At the far end of this field you come up via a zigzag to a stone wall and slate stile which leads you into a wild bracken area.

Now you are looking across at a two-storey building, strangely called the Manor House. Meanwhile, the Coast Path bends back, keeping to the seaward side of the Manor House. Ladies Window is a natural archway on the western side of a small headland just to the seaward side of the Coast Path. It overlooks a deep, inaccessible cove. Continuing west you will see Long and Short Islands, the largest colony of puffins in Cornwall. The caravan site across the bay is on the former Borough Farm, the centre of the old rotten borough of Bossiney.

Looking across the bay you can see the enormous hotel at Tintagel on the headland in the distance. At the camp site that you now reach, an ideal camping location for Coast Path walkers, keep to the seaward side of the caravans. Just west of all this you come to the Rocky Valley, a very deep gulley with a small river running through the middle. The path goes down steps on both sides and crosses a footbridge.

Contours are given in metres
The vertical interval is 10m

To the west of the Rocky Valley you overlook Benoath Cove and Bossiney Haven. There are a number of caves here. At Bossiney Haven there is a pierced rock often referred to as the elephant rock because of its resemblance to an elephant's trunk. A side path down to Benoath Beach descends the cliff next to a bench near the cliff top. There is a warning pointing out that the path is steep and slippery and should be used with caution. It also states that is is not suitable for children. Benoath is a small, sandy beach, safe for bathing on incoming tides only. Make local enquiries about tides.

As you come out above Bossiney Haven you will see the elephant rock below you and the small sandy beach. Cross the steep track, up which packhorses used to bring sand and seaweed to spread on the local fields.

Now the Coast Path cuts across another promontory. This is also called Willapark, although only 2 miles (3 km) from the other Willapark, and is a fort too. The remains are difficult to make out and are partly incorporated in the field boundary across the neck of the headland.

The puffins, razorbills and guillemots (of the auk family) spend most of their year far out to sea. Should you be lucky enough to be here during the breeding season, a good pair of binoculars will enable you to see all three species of these beautiful birds flying between their nests and their fishing grounds and sitting on the water below the clifftop path ready to dive for fish. The puffin has its brightly coloured beak only during the nesting season.

The land is all National Trust property and you are welcome to explore the cliff tops. After Willapark you come to Gullastem, a wide cove with a rocky beach, which is not easily accessible. The path skirts round, keeping fairly close to the top of the cliff here.

The Coast Path continues close to the cliff edge, sometimes passing under the higher parts of Smith's Cliff. All along this stretch you will hear the pounding of powerful waves against the cliffs below. Crossing a small stone stile to the west of Gullastem you come to the National Trust notice for Barras Nose and the Victorian mock-Gothic, King Arthur Castle Hotel can be seen just inland. Now the path brings you to Tintagel Haven. Keep an eye open for the resident seals which may come to have a look at you.

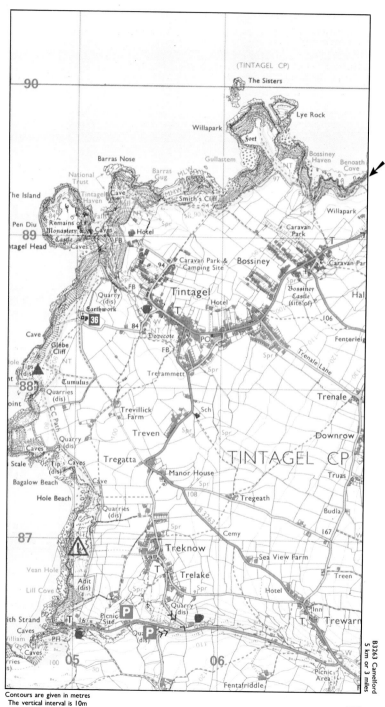

Contours are given in metres
The vertical interval is 10m

From the Stone Age to Christianity on the North Cornish coast

Flint implements show that Stone Age man was here. Evidence that Bronze Age people also inhabited the area is provided by their burial mounds (tumuli), a method of burial that seems to have lasted for the 1,500 years following 2500 BC.

The Bronze Age people, of course, exploited and traded quantities of copper and tin. Both minerals are present in Cornwall. As a result, it is suggested that there was trade contact between Cornwall and the Mediterranean from very early times.

During the Iron Age, promontory forts were built all along the Coast Path, and the Romans left us the inscribed stones which can be seen at Trevethey, and in Tintagel Church.

Early Christianity, represented here by the Celtic Church, was very much based on the monastery. It seems that to become a saint in the Celtic Church was mainly a matter of leading a holy life and taking a pilgrimage to convert heathens, which would have involved founding new religious settlements and churches. The pilgrim who did this may have given his or her name to the church concerned.

Cornwall has many links with the Celtic past of Europe. It was not until the late 18th century that the last person to speak Cornish as a first language died. The language is closely related to Welsh and to the Breton still spoken in Brittany, and more distantly to those of the Gaeltacht areas of Ireland, and to the Gaelic of the Scottish Highlands. The legend of King Arthur (see page 138) is shared by these countries but it is in Cornwall that it still seems to have the strongest hold.

Tintagel Haven

Small trading vessels would have called regularly at this haven from earliest times until the late 19th century. Remember that this would have been a small settlement and that the buildings would have been inhabited cottages.

Note the round platform on the opposite side of the cove from the castle. There are pictures of how this structure was used in King Arthur's Hall in the village. Just below it is the place where ships would have been tied up for loading and unloading. The main export would have been slate, some of it from the quarries of Glebe Cliff just round the corner.

It is difficult nowadays to imagine these tiny ports in their heyday when regular loads of slates, often stacked and carried into the holds of the ships by women, would have left for destinations all over South Wales and the West of England, and even, occasionally, much further afield.

Tintagel

The name Tintagel originally applied to the headland on which the castle stands, and the area around the church and Glebe Cliff. As a result of the 19th century fascination with Arthurian legend, Tintagel Castle had become famous and so the settlement known until that date as Trevena was renamed Tintagel in order to increase the hamlet's tourist attraction.

When in Tintagel, you may wish to visit the Hall of Chivalry and King Arthur's Hall, now used for Masonic meetings. The most striking building in the village, however, is undoubtedly the Old Post Office, used as such in the 19th century, but really a 14th or 15th century house. Inside you can see the original hall and its gallery and screens passage. It is now owned by the National Trust.

Tintagel Castle

The site is outstandingly beautiful. A series of excavations in the 1930s brought to light pottery of the 4th to 7th centuries, which we now know originated in North Africa, Turkey and Greece. There is also evidence, from the Roman stone in Tintagel Church and another similar one near St Piran's Well, that the Romans were here. Cornwall was probably producing substantial quantities of tin at the time. This could well have been the export that rendered the local community wealthy enough to import luxury goods from the Mediterranean.

Clearly, these inhabitants of the peninsula, on which a castle was built at a considerably later time, were rich, and we may draw the conclusion that they may also have been powerful. The archaeological evidence also suggests that the site was deserted by the 8th century, and the first written mention of Tintagel is by Geoffrey of Monmouth in his semi-fictional *History of the Kings of Britain*, published some four centuries later in the late 1130s. Perhaps some local oral tradition that Tintagel Castle had once been the stronghold of wealthy Celtic inhabitants of Cornwall led him to link the story of a powerful and goodly king of the distant past with this promontory.

The style of the ruins suggests a 12th or 13th century date. In other words, the castle you see now was actually built after

Geoffrey of Monmouth wrote his book. Perhaps the decision of the Norman rulers of Britain to site a castle on this spot was more an act of symbolic acknowledgement of its supposed glorious past than an act of strategic military importance.

King Arthur and the Knights of the Round Table

Did King Arthur really exist? If he did, who did he represent and how has this most intriguing of Celtic legends been handed down to us over the centuries?

One suggestion is that a number of kings or leaders emerged in Britain to fill the vacuum caused by the departure of the Romans. These leaders had to defend the island against invaders, including the Saxons. Feats of great bravery were no doubt enacted in the course of these struggles. We know that Ambrosius Aurelianus checked the advance of the Saxons towards the end of the 5th century. Some people think that a verbal tradition of a King Arthur may have been based on Ambrosius Aurelianus himself.

It is difficult to be sure of any of the events of this period. Virtually all the scribes were monks, who took little interest in secular affairs. One sketchy clue is based on a document called *De Excidio Britanniae* (on the destruction of Britain) by a Celtic monk called Gildas. It never mentions Arthur, but does attempt to give a brief history of the British from the departure of the Romans until the time of Ambrosius Aurelianus. He writes about a battle at Mons Badonicus which is deemed to have taken place at the very end of the 5th century. The document was probably written about half a century later. The leader of the battle is not named, and we have no means of knowing where Mons Badonicus was or is.

The next reference is by a monk called Nennius in his *History of the Britons*, written late in the 9th century, 300 years after the events he claims to be recording, and he names an Arthur as a victor in battle.

In the 12th century, Geoffrey of Monmouth took the whole story a stage further by suggesting, on the flimsiest of evidence, that Arthur was a great British king and a historic figure, at a time when the legend, embellished through the ages of verbal recounting, was developing and forming the basis of many literary epics. When printing found its way to Europe, the story found an ever wider audience, and the codes of chivalry helped to boost the appeal of the epic. The supposed connections with various localities in each of the Celtic countries of Western

Europe are all as unlikely and unfounded as each other, and Geoffrey of Monmouth's chosen setting of Tintagel falls into this category. However, it is a wonderful story and has supplied good entertainment for centuries, and some marvellous literature in several languages. A clifftop castle such as Tintagel is as good a setting as any, even if it was not built until several centuries after the story first emerged!

Tintagel Church

Tintagel Church **36** (see map on page 135) was built at the turn of the 11th and 12th centuries, shortly after the arrival of William the Conqueror, when the land here was held, then as now, by the Dukes of Cornwall.

There is a Norman font, a 15th century rood screen, a reredos behind the altar made of the old bench-ends, and the Roman stone in the south transept. This is often referred to as a milestone, which it is not. It stood by the church stile until 1888 and was used to rest coffins on and to sharpen reap hooks and knives. Then it was noticed that it had a Latin inscription with the abbreviated name of the Roman Emperor Licinius, who was put to death by the Emperor Constantine after a disagreement in AD 324. The stone may have been put up to mark the authority of the Roman Empire in this area.

Inside Tintagel Castle's ruins.

12 Tintagel Haven to Portgaverne

via Trebarwith Strand
7½ miles (12.2 km)

From Tintagel Haven the Coast Path official route runs upstream briefly and then zigzags right (south-west) to the top of
the steep valley edge. A seal may greet you swimming around
the cove. As you come away from the upper ward of Tintagel
Castle, you enter National Trust land, Glebe Cliff, and can in
practice follow any of the clifftop routes that criss-cross the area.
The official route keeps just back from the cliff top and more or
less parallel to it all the way to Trebarwith Strand, crossing a
couple of meadows just south of the youth hostel and then
remaining outside field boundaries all the way to Trebarwith.

You may wish to visit the medieval church and have a quick
look at the clifftop slate quarries (see page 146) just south of the
youth hostel. Between Tregatta and Trebarwith you will pass
more cliff-face quarries, including Tria **37**, Bagalow **38**, and
Lanterdan **39**, the last with a distinctive stone pillar. The extent
of mediaeval building in the immediate vicinity means that
quarrying would have been taking place here in the Middle
Ages and it continued until the 1930s. Take extreme care not to
stray too near any of the cliff-faces here. Just south of the
quarries you will see a seat, and soon after this the path starts to
descend steeply beside the ancient donkey track from Treknow
to emerge on the road at Trebarwith Strand (see page 148).

Swimming is often dangerous in this area because of the
strong currents and tides. People are drowned every year
because of this. In unsupervised coves, you should bathe only
on the incoming tide from sandy beaches before the tide rises
high enough to reach the rocks. On supervised beaches, such as
Trebarwith Strand, it is extremely important to obey the notices
displayed by the lifeguards on the blackboard and the safe-
bathing flag system. Tide tables are published by North Cornwall District Council and are on display in local public places,
youth hostels, hotels and local pubs.

To continue south and west along the Coast Path, go to the
landward end of the Port William public house and turn left to
follow the zigzagging track uphill, starting off by going some
yards inland. A sharp hairpin bend soon takes you back
towards the cliff top. Go up the straight set of steps to the top of
Dennis Point. When you reach this, follow the cliff initially,

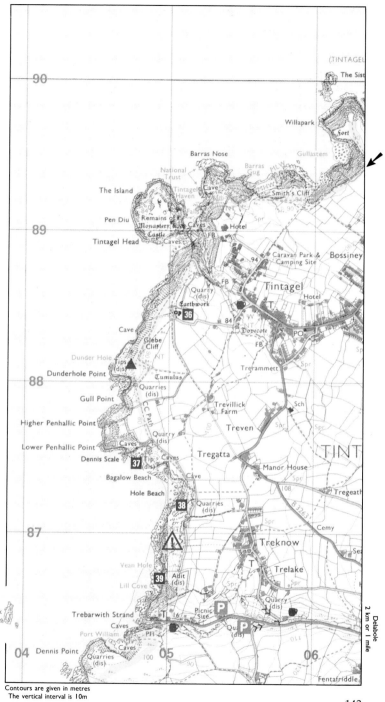

Contours are given in metres
The vertical interval is 10m

143

keeping straight on (south-west) to cut across Dennis Point. You have just risen from sea level to 300 feet (100 metres) and are about to drop to sea level once again at Backways Cove. There are five steep drops and rises similar to the ones you see before you in the 6 miles (10 km) to Port Isaac, so you should allow five hours to reach there from Trebarwith Strand.

From the cliff top at Dennis Point, descend into a beautifully secluded and quiet valley where a small stream runs into the cove. Then climb back up and follow the cliff top west along Treligga Cliff.

The Coast Path stays on the cliff top all the way from Trebarwith Strand to Portgaverne, but there are one or two places where some description will help you avoid landing up on the beach or going inland. Just south of the National Trust Tregardock sign, 'The Mountain' – a steep little peak isolated by erosion all round – comes into sight, standing above Tregardock Beach. Keep alongside the fence at the top of the steep slope **A**, until you see the path zigzag down towards the stream and cross a footbridge. The paths shown on the map here do not exist on the ground and so some care needs to be taken. To the seaward side you will see a path that goes south of The Mountain. This leads to the beach. Another path leads inland, upstream to Tregardock. The Coast Path strikes south up the steep bank and soon returns to the top of Tregardock Cliff, where there used to be a lead and silver mine.

After Tregardock the path remains on the cliff top for half a mile (1 km) to Jacket's Point. Continue south on the cliff top. Once you have left the National Trust land, the field boundaries are often extremely close to the cliff and those suffering from vertigo would be ill-advised to walk this section. At Jacket's Point, you will see that the Coast Path descends once more almost to sea level, keeping quite close to the cliff edge, which it does on the southern side of the valley as well, passing a dramatic, deep, surging creek as it does so. Having reached the top you stay on the plateau for only about 300 yards (275 metres) before dropping once again almost to sea level, having crossed a stile at the top of the slope to come inside the fields where the path remains until Pigeon's Cove.

As the path rises out of the valley on the southern side, you will pass a disused tunnel, once used by donkeys to carry slate to the beach to be loaded onto ships (marked 'Adit' on the map) **40**. Take great care on the cliff edge, which is eroding very rapidly.

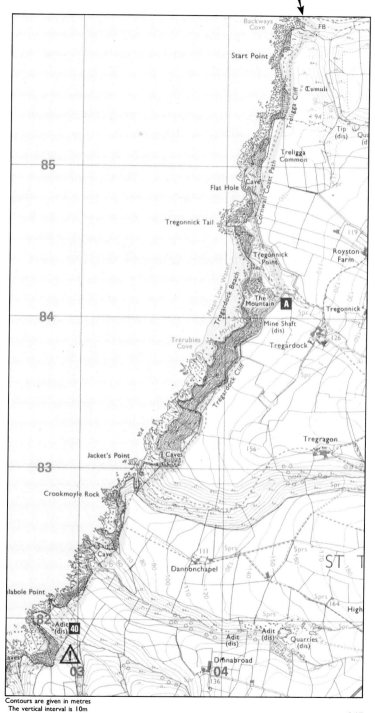

Backways Cove
FB
Start Point
Treligga Cliff
Tumuli
94
Tip (dis)
Qu (d
Treligga Common
Spr
119
Cave
Flat Hole
Cornwall Coast Path
Tregonnick Tail
Royston Farm
Tregonnick Point
Main Low Water
Tregardock Beach
The Mountain
A
Tregonnick
Spr
MHW
Mine Shaft (dis)
126
Trerubies Cove
Tregardock
Tregardock Cliff
Spr
Tregragon
Jacket's Point
156
Caves
83
Crookmoyle Rock
Sprs
Sprs
ST T
Cave
111
Sprs
Dannonchapel
164
High
abole Point
Adit (dis)
40
Adit (dis)
Adit (dis)
Quarries (dis)
⚠
03
Dinnabroad
04
136

Contours are given in metres
The vertical interval is 10m

145

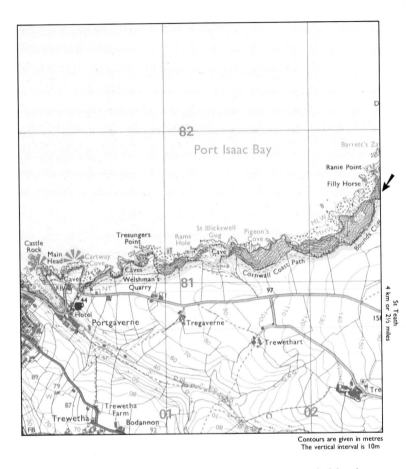

Contours are given in metres
The vertical interval is 10m

Continue along the cliff top, keeping inside the fields along Bounds Cliff. The path here is reasonably level until just west of Pigeon's Cove, where you come into sight of St Illickswell Gug. Here you will see that the Coast Path goes outside the fence and dips down into the small valley below, clinging to the clifftop slopes above Rams Hole, before returning to the cliff top for the remainder of the way to Portgaverne, a former slate port and fishing village (see page 148).

The slate quarries at Tintagel

If you are coming from the north, the first quarry you will see clearly is just below the youth hostel. Just north of the youth hostel is Long Grass Quarry and in the little bay just south of it, Lambshouse Cove, are Lambshouse Quarry and Gull Point Quarry.

If you look across Lambshouse Cove, from the sloping slate platform below the youth hostel, you can see a round slate platform perched at the top of the cliff with a smaller square platform just below it. The round platform is the site of a donkey whim.

In the centre of the circle was a post set in a revolving socket. Placed on top of this post, like an old-fashioned tap handle, would be a second bar that made the central post revolve. When the central post was turned by a donkey, a chain or rope would wind around it, hauling a load of slate or a returning quarry-face worker up the cliff. In the mines, the rope or chain would have passed down the mine-shaft.

In many of the smaller ports of Cornwall you can see similar traces of the arrangements devised for pulling the ships up the beach, out of reach of dangerous waves, or for loading the boats from the quay or cliff edge.

One of the slate-quarrying platforms between Tintagel and Treknow.

The remains of one such whim can be seen opposite Merlin's Cave and the castle at Tintagel Haven, and a similar, more daring arrangement can be seen if you go along the narrow clifftop path for a short distance south of the youth hostel, around Lambshouse Cove and out to Penhallic Point.

You can go down to the disused wharf at Penhallic Point (see map on page 143) if you have a head for heights, but you get a better view of how it might have worked if you keep to the clifftop path a little longer and look at it across the small cove to the south. From here you can see the zigzag cart track along which the slates were brought in donkey carts. To hold the boats steady against the Atlantic swell, ropes were connected to rings set in the rocks below and in the cliff, and the loads were then let down 100 feet (30 metres) into the boats below.

Long Grass Quarry, next to the youth hostel, was worked until 50 years ago and the quarry buildings and office are now the Tintagel Youth Hostel.

Port William and Trebarwith Strand

Port William, still shown on the maps, was a harbour from which slates were exported in large quantities well into the last century.

Imagine the donkeys and carts coming down and the waiting sailing boats pulled up on the beach being loaded with slates by the local women wearing their Cornish bonnets.

Mrs Thomas Hardy refers in her diaries to visiting Trebarwith Strand in the early 1870s, 'where donkeys were employed carrying seaweed to the farmers'. You can still see the cut along which these donkeys would have reached the beach, running parallel with the miniature gorge that carries the stream down to the sea.

Portgaverne

The road by which you approach Portgaverne from the east is the Great Slate Road. This was quarried out in 1807 at the expense of the Delabole Slate Company to enable the slate carts to reach this small haven. They were drawn by horses or oxen, and one method of braking used to slow their descent down this hill was to run the wheels along the wall. If you look at the wall opposite the Headlands Hotel, you can still see the grooves they made. The road was finished in 1860. Old photos show that many of the people who helped with the loading were women. Two cargoes a week left during the latter part of the 19th century. Records show that slate went to Barnstaple, Bristol and the Continent direct from Portgaverne. When the railway came, in 1897, the port suffered from a major depression. The women who had loaded the slates in the past frequently dug sand and loaded it on to carts for use in the fields, and other people in the village turned to agriculture.

In addition to the slate, Portgaverne was also a fishing village. The usual method was seining, which involved a number of boats going out to a shoal of fish and gradually working the nets around them until they were surrounded.

As you arrive at the beach of Portgaverne you will see a house opposite called Chimneys. This was the Salting House for the method then used to preserve fish. The blacksmith's forge, where all the beasts of burden would have been shod, was in the dwelling now known as the Beach House, and in addition there used to be four cellars to which the landed fish were taken. It is said that at the beginning of the last century one of these cellars could handle more than 1.5 million fish during a good autumn fishing week. Most of the fish cellars are now used as holiday accommodation.

Fish and slate were not the only cargoes to be brought to Portgaverne. There was also limestone, for Portgaverne had its lime kiln, and the ships would also bring coal, general supplies and manure for the farmers. Portgaverne in addition had its own boatbuilding yards.

It was impossible for larger boats to turn around safely in the port, so an ingenious method was worked out to pull them out backwards by means of ropes and chains passed through metal rings set in rocks just outside the harbour. This method was called 'warping out'.

Until the late 19th century, most of the slate from the massive Delabole Quarry was shipped via Portgaverne in the summer and from Boscastle, which had better shelter, in the winter. The slate would have been exported mainly by boat until the arrival of the railways. These days it goes by road.

The Quay at Rock.

13 Portgaverne to Padstow

through Port Isaac and Portquin
12¼ miles (19.8 km)

Going from Portgaverne westwards, you follow the pavement on the road towards Port Isaac until you come to the car park at the top of the hill and then you keep to the cliff top. There are buses from Port Isaac to Wadebridge about every two hours on weekdays.

(Coming from the west, to get from Port Isaac to Portgaverne, pass the harbour, go up the hill past the old school which is now a hotel, and follow the very narrow street going along the cliff top and overlooking the harbour.)

To follow the Coast Path west of Port Isaac and towards Padstow, go to the southern side of the harbour and up the narrow lane, Roscarrock Hill, which leads up past the Wesleyan chapel. Go to the end of this road and turn right, along the cliffs just before the guesthouses that face you. This path soon brings you to the clifftop fields. Skirt around the headland, Lobber Point, and coming through the wall you will get a fine view of Varley Head and, a few yards later, of Pine Haven.

Portgavèrne fish cellars.

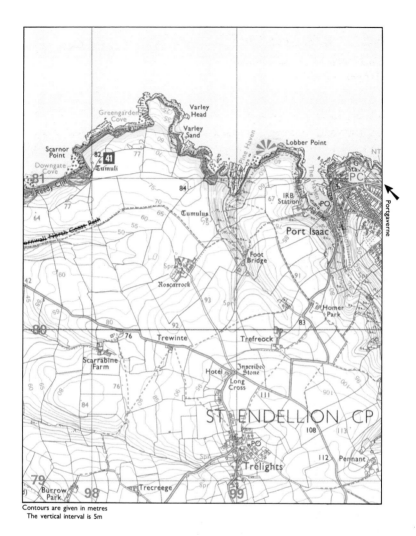

Contours are given in metres
The vertical interval is 5m

A stiff climb brings you out of Pine Haven towards Varley Head. After passing through a barbed-wire corridor, the path goes behind Greengarden Cove, where there is a Napoleonic cannon on top of a mound, and then round to Scarnor Point. As the path turns west to go down steps around Downgate Cove, note the two surviving Bronze Age tumuli **41** in the adjacent fields.

The securely fenced path continues along the back of Downgate Cove, with the fence almost becoming a work of art as it winds in and out and stretches the half-mile (1 km) to Kellan Head.

The well-protected natural harbour at Portquin, with Doyden Point and Doyden Castle.

As you round Kellan Head, where there used to be a coast-guard lookout, you will come within sight of the natural harbour of Portquin. On the headland immediately to the west of Portquin, Doyden Point, stands the folly called Doyden Castle **42**. This was built by one Samuel Symmons, shortly after he bought the headland in 1827, as a place where he and his friends could have a good time drinking and gambling. Just behind it is Doyden House, built by an ex-governor of Wandsworth Prison as his retirement home.

You will come into Portquin between a large, double-chimneyed, stone house and a white-painted cottage, down a flight of slate steps. Make your way along the back of the beach noting the slots in the walls of the fish cellars, which were used for weighting and compressing the pilchards during the salting process. Continue up the road until you see a stile. Turn right over the stile, branching seawards around the prison governor's house, and make for the fenced shafts **43** on the cliff top towards Gilson's Cove ahead. These are the old antimony mines which, with the pilchard fishing, were the livelihood of the people of

Portquin for many years.

(If you are coming from the west, go to the clifftop stile on the road down to Portquin. Turn left down the road and look for the gap between the stone houses and the whitewashed stone cottage. Go between the two, forking left where a staircase goes in each direction, and then follow the cliff to Port Isaac.)

From the old mine shafts at Doyden the path stays just to the seaward side of the field boundary, going past Pigeon Cove and up to Trevan Point, which stands 200 feet (60 metres) high. From Trevan Point there is a fine view of Epphaven Cove and Lundy Beach. Here there is sand at low tide, caves and rock pools, all the ingredients of an idyllic Cornish cove. The intriguing natural arch called Lundy Hole **44** was once a cave, the roof of which has collapsed. There is a car park on the road a quarter of a mile (400 metres) inland.

Continue west behind the cliff to Carnweather Point and round the back of Downhedge Cove. The quarry **45** just west of the cove was used for the extraction of greenstone for local building and road surfacing. Carry on westwards round the back of Pengirt Cove and past the tips of the disused lead mine,

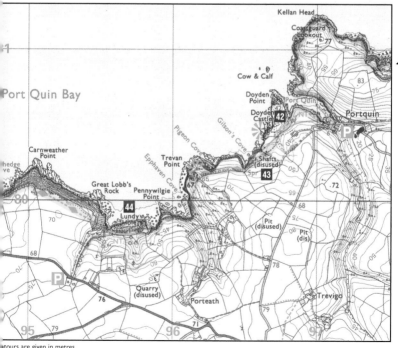

tours are given in metres
he vertical interval is 5m

now used to hide a car park. This mine was in production at various times from the 16th century until the end of the 19th. Now go around the landward side of Com Head from which there are fine views.

You are now going north-west towards the Iron Age fort on the promontory known as The Rumps **46**. Note the banks, which are the fortifications, on the landward side. Excavation has shown that the earth banks were originally faced with stone. The point where the footpath goes through was originally a complex defensive entrance which led to the headland, where there would have been circular wooden huts. The excavation also showed that our Iron Age ancestors wove the wool from their sheep to make clothes, were expert fishermen, and cultivated some grain crops. They had sufficient surplus income to buy their pottery elsewhere, and it would appear that they were buying Mediterranean wine and pottery.

From The Rumps, continue south-west to Pentire Point, from where you have a fine view of Padstow Bay. Stepper Point is the opposite headland forming the entrance to the bay, and Trevose Head, with its lighthouse, can be seen further away. On the way from The Rumps you may have seen outcrops of 'pillow lava' forced up through the sea floor when the other rocks of this area were being formed. The sea water caused rapid cooling, making the formation pile up as you now see it, and the gases in the lava forced their way out, leaving holes and channels as they escaped. Now turn south-east towards Polzeath.

The National Trust has owned all this land since 1936, when a speculator divided the whole of the Pentire headland into building plots and put them up for sale. Money was collected to buy all the land which was presented to the National Trust, who have since completed purchases of the cliff top all the way to Portquin. At Pentireglaze Haven, skirt round the haven on the cliff top and join the road for a short stretch in New Polzeath.

Stay on the top of the cliff and keep behind the last few houses by the small stream, taking to the road again past the shops at Polzeath. Go between the houses at the southern side of the beach just opposite Polzeath Methodist Church. Then keep along the cliff top and cross the beach at Daymer Bay, or keep to the path in the dunes at high tide. Follow the path around the seaward side of Brea Hill.

When people first came to this area, the sea level was very much lower, and only 6,000 years ago it would have been about 20 feet (6 metres) below present levels. Padstow Bay is one of the

Contours are given in metres
The vertical interval is 5m

157

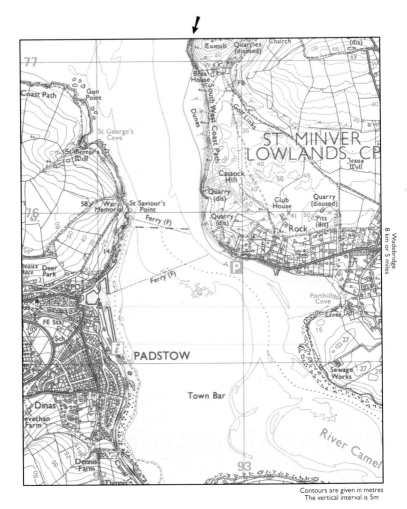

Contours are given in metres
The vertical interval is 5m

places along your walk where at very low tides you may still see the fossilised relics of tree stumps, which are all that remains of the forests of that era.

Now make your way along the beach or through the dunes until you come to the car park at the end of the road at Rock. The ferry here runs virtually every day of the year except Sundays in winter, but when the tide is low it may drop you a little downstream of Padstow, leaving you to return along the banks of the River Camel if you wish to visit Padstow before continuing your walk along the South West Coast Path, using National Trail Guide no. 9.

A circular walk: Portquin and Port Isaac
5 miles (7.9 km)

Park at the National Trust car park at Portquin, and walk inland back up the valley (east) until you see a green and white sign that says 'Footpath to Port Isaac 2 miles'. Follow this direction past the cottage and over a stone stile beside a white gate. Keep straight on up the valley. After 500 yards (450 metres) it opens out and the path forks left, away from the stream, towards a stile between two gates. Go over this stile and continue along the farm track which follows the field boundaries, eventually curving round to the right (south-east). Pass just north of Roscarrock Farm. When you reach the field where you can see the farm quite closely on your right, with the track you have been following going down to it, turn left (north-east) and away from the farm.

At the far end of the field you will find a stile overlooking Pine Haven. Once over the stile branch right (north-east), drop down to the valley, and cross a stream by a footbridge. Then go diagonally up the hill opposite. When you get to the top of the steep slope, branch left, slightly away from the wall you have been following, to pass a white mast on the ridge of the hill.

Make for a stone stile in the field boundary facing you, after which you stay close to the upper side of the boundary which becomes a small sunken lane. You will emerge on to the road above Port Isaac harbour. Turn right if you want to go into Port Isaac or left, and along the cliffs, if you wish to follow the Coast Path back to Portquin. Along the Coast Path, skirt around Lobber Point, then climb out of Pine Haven to pass Greengarden Cove and Scarnor Point, continuing towards Kellan Head. From here you will walk back to Portquin and the car park.

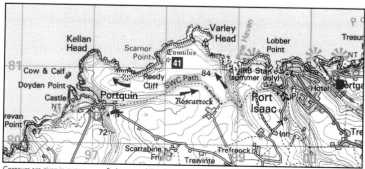

Contours are given in metres
The vertical interval is 10m
Scale approx 1¼ inches to 1 mile

159

Polzeath Beach, a fine stretch of sand and a surfer's paradise from dawn to dusk.

PART THREE

Useful
Information

Transport

Rail

For Minehead go via Taunton where you take the bus, normally to Minehead but better still to Bishop's Lydeard, and then on the West Somerset Railway if it is running that day. (For Talking Timetable and further information Tel. 01643 707650.)

There are services to Exeter from all parts of Britain. There is a choice of services via London Waterloo (a two-hourly service), a frequent London Paddington service, and good services from Bristol, Taunton and Westbury. Change at Exeter St Davids. From there to Barnstaple there is a two-hourly service on the Tarka line from Monday to Saturday, rather less frequent on Sundays in the winter. There are daily through services, avoiding London, to and from all other parts of the country. For timetable and fare information, phone 0345 484950 (24-hour service).

Buses

Getting there and back

There are normally *daily* express services by coach from all parts of the country to Taunton, Exeter, Barnstaple and Bude. Tickets for these services should be bought in advance from travel agents or from offices of the company concerned. For enquiries see 'National Express' in your local phone book.

Using buses for day walks

There are all-year-round services operating in the Minehead–Hartland sector, with buses using the main roads, which are never far from the coast, and regular stops at all the coastal towns and villages along the route.

Local Tourist Information Centres can supply free copies of the Exmoor and West Somerset and the North Devon Public Transport Guides, or phone ATMOS Ltd (Somerset County Council) on 01823 358232 or Devon County Council on 01392 382800 for timetable information. Summer timetables are normally available from the end of May each year and winter timetables from the end of October. Likewise in North Cornwall the Heritage Coast Service issues a leaflet summarising the bus services that are useful to coastal walkers, available from the tourist information centres there and from Boscastle Visitor Centre Tel. 01840 250010. Small local private firms run many of the services.

Getting up steam on the West Somerset Railway at Minehead, one way to arrive in traditional style to start the great walk.

163

For times of Western National buses and National Express Services write to them at Union Street, Camborne, Cornwall, TR14 8HF or phone 01208 79898.

Ferries
The ferry from Instow to Appledore operates, subject to tides, in high season only.

The Bideford or Ilfracombe to Lundy ferry services operate throughout the year – roughly speaking, every few days in the early spring and late autumn, and every other day or daily in season, and at some time each week in winter. Timetables and tickets are available from all local tourist information centres, and a 24-hour answering service at Bideford Quay 01237 470422 gives details, or you can make bookings during office hours.

The Padstow–Rock ferry operates when required, virtually every day of the year except Sundays in winter during reasonable daylight hours. There is also a separately operated evening water taxi operating '8 till late' – to book phone 01208 862815 during daytime or 01208 862217 evenings.

Accommodation contacts

The Ramblers' Association yearbook and the South West Way Association guidebook – both published annually – list bed and breakfast places. See pages 165 and 166.

All the local tourist information centres can find you accommodation, including booking ahead bed and breakfast accommodation along your route. They try to make reservations for the time you ask, but if you leave this until the last minute during the school holiday periods you may have to go some distance inland. The centres are also well stocked with information about places to visit nearby, and in addition to free leaflets they sell pamphlets and guides. The staff can suggest places to go for a day out, and direct you to heritage coast guided walks.

For camping see Ordnance Survey maps in this guide or ask at the tourist information centres below. The following centres are affiliated to the West Country Tourist Board, 60 St Davids Hill, Exeter, Devon, EX4 4QS. Tel. 01392 276351.

The Tourist Information Centre, 36 Boutport Street, Barnstaple, Devon, EX31 1RX. Tel. 01271 375000.
The Tourist Information Centre, Victoria Park, The Quay, Bideford, Devon, EX39 2QQ. Tel. 01237 477676.
The Tourist Information Centre, The Crescent Car Park, Bude,

Cornwall, EX23 8LE. Tel. 01288 354240.

The Tourist Information Centre, North Cornwall Museum, The Clease, Camelford, Cornwall, PL32 9PL. Tel. 01840 212954 (seasonal).

The Tourist Information Centre, The Bakehouse Centre, Caen Street, Braunton.

The Tourist Information Centre, Seacot, Cross Street, Combe Martin, Devon, EX34 0DH. Tel. 01271 883319 (seasonal).

The Tourist Information Centre, The Landmark, Ilfracombe, Devon, EX34 9BX. Tel. 01271 863001.

The Tourist Information Centre, The Town Hall, Lee Road, Lynton, Devon, EX35 6BT. Tel. 01598 752225.

The Tourist Information Centre, 17 Friday Street, Minehead, Somerset, TA24 5UB. Tel. 01643 702624.

The Tourist Information Centre, Red Brick Building, North Quay, Padstow, Cornwall, PL28 8AF. Tel. 01841 533449 (seasonal).

The Tourist Information Centre, Red Barn Car Park, Barton Road, Woolacombe, Devon. Tel. 01271 870553 (seasonal).

Visitor Centres

The Tarka Trail Visitor Centre, Bideford Station (on the route), Railway Terrace, East-the-Water, Bideford, Devon, EX39 4BB. Tel. 01237 471870.

Boscastle Visitor Centre, excellent displays and information about the North Cornwall Heritage Coast – in the main car park and open 7 days a week 10.30 a.m.–5 p.m. throughout the year. Tel. 01840 250010.

Bude Visitor Centre provides information about the local natural history of the area, combined with TIC (see above).

Exmoor National Park Visitor Centre, The Esplanade, Lynmouth, Devon, EX35 6EQ. Tel. 01598 752509.

Other contacts

The Association of Lightweight Campers, c/o The Camping and Caravanning Club, Greenfields House, Westwood Way, Coventry, CV4 7JA. Tel. 01203 694995.

The Ramblers' Association, 1–5 Wandsworth Road, London, SW8 2XX. Tel. 0171 339 8500. (Handbook has many bed and breakfast addresses: available free to members; available to non-members from major bookshops and newsagents for $4.99 or + $1.00 p&p if ordered direct from the RA.)

The Youth Hostels Association, Trevelyan House, 8 St Stephen's Hill, St Albans, Herts, AL1 2DY. Tel. 01727 855215.

Local organisations

You may like to join, or make a contribution or donation to, one of the local organisations that helps to look after the coast.

Coastal conservation and management are expensive these days, so even if you are already a member of the organisation concerned please put some money in the box if you have enjoyed the magnificent scenery which they are helping to protect. When added together these small donations all help the cause.

The Cornwall Wildlife Trust, Five Acres, Allet, Truro, Cornwall, TR4 9DJ. Tel. 01872 273939.

Devon Wildlife Trust, 35 St Davids Hill, Exeter, Devon, EX4 4DA. Tel. 01392 79244.

The South West Way Association, Membership Secretary, 25 Clobells, South Brent, Devon, TQ10 9JW. Tel/Fax: 01364 73859. The South West Way Association exists to help those who enjoy walking this path. For advice and about the Coast Path, phone Eric Wallis on (01752) 896237.

Other useful addresses

North Devon Coast and Countryside Service, Old Bideford Station, Bideford East, EX39 4BB. Tel. 01237 423655.

Countryside Commission (Headquarters), John Dower House, Crescent Place, Cheltenham, Glos, GL50 3RA. Tel. 01242 521381.

Countryside Commission, South West Regional Office, Bridge House, Sion Place, Clifton, Bristol, BS8 4AS. Tel. 0117 9739966.

Exmoor National Park Authority, Exmoor House, Dulverton, Somerset, TA22 9HL. Tel. 01398 323665.

National Trust, Cornwall Regional Office, Lanhydrock House, Bodmin, Cornwall, PL30 4DE. Tel. 01208 74281.

National Trust, Devon Regional Office, Killerton House, Broadclyst, Exeter, EX5 3LE. Tel. 01392 881691.

English Nature, Somerset Team, Roughmoor, Bishop's Hull, Taunton, TA1 5AA. Tel. 01823 283211.

English Nature, Devon and Cornwall Team, The Old Mill House, 37 North Street, Okehampton, Devon, EX20 1AR. Tel. 01837 55045.

North Cornwall Heritage Coast and Countryside Service, 3/5 Barn Lane, Bodmin, Cornwall, PL31 1LZ. Tel. 01208 74121.

Ordnance Survey, Romsey Road, Maybush, Southampton, SO9 4DH. Tel. 01703 792912.

Royal Society for the Protection of Birds, The Lodge, Sandy, Beds, SG19 2GL. Tel. 01767 680551. (Regional office: Keble House, Southernhay Gardens, Exeter, EX1 1NT. Tel. 01392 432691.

South West Coast Path Team, c/o Devon County Council, County Hall, Exeter, EX2 4QW. Tel. 01392 383560.

Guided walks

Many guided walks are now conducted along the route of the path. These are led by local experts and can add a completely new dimension to a holiday on this coast. The normal duration is a couple of hours. Copies of the programmes may be obtained from the tourist information centres above, national park and heritage coast visitor centres, public libraries and museums. Some walks are organised privately, others by local civic and naturalists' societies. Many in this area are organised by the Heritage Coast Service and Exmoor National Park Authority.

Nearby places of interest

Arlington Court – stately home of the Chichester family. *Gypsy Moth IV* model, carriage collection and other memorabilia in wonderful gardens.

Camelford – North Cornwall Museum – mining, quarrying, and North Cornwall mining exhibits and history.

Trebarwith/Trewarmett – Prince of Wales Quarry – wildlife and restored engine house.

Bibliography

Aird, Alisdair, *The Good Pub Guide* (Vermilion, annually).

Barber, Richard, *King Arthur in Legend and History* (Cardinal, 1973).

Coleridge, Samuel Taylor, *Kubla Khan* and *The Rime of the Ancient Mariner*.

Court, Glyn, *Exmoor National Park Countryside Commission Official Guide* (Michael Joseph, 1986).

Delderfield, E. R., *The Lynmouth Flood Disaster* (E. R. D. Publications, 1969).

Devon and Exmoor, Leisure Guide (A A and Ordnance Survey, 1988).

Exmoor and the Quantocks, Pathfinder Guide (Ordnance Survey and Jarrolds, 1990).

Gittings, Robert, *Young Thomas Hardy* (Penguin, 1978).

Grinsell, L. V., *The Archaeology of Exmoor* (David & Charles).

Hall, Jean, *Railway Landmarks in Devon* (David & Charles, 1982).

Hardy, Thomas, *A Pair of Blue Eyes* (Macmillan, 1873 and 1975).

Kingsley, Charles, *Westward Ho!* (Heron).

Lawrence, B., *Coleridge and Wordsworth in Somerset* (David & Charles).

Madge, Robin, *Railways Round Exmoor* (Exmoor Press, Dulverton, 1988).

National Trust leaflet series on the Devon and Cornwall coasts.

North Cornwall Heritage Coast and Coast Path leaflet series, *Coastlines* annual free newspaper publication plus guides to town and village trails, the seashore, geology and wildlife.

North Devon, Exmoor and the Quantocks Landranger Guidebook (OS and Jarrold, 1989).

Pevsner, N., *North Devon* and *Cornwall* (Penguin Buildings of England Series).

Soper, Tony, *Guide to the Coast* (National Trust and Webb & Bower).

Thomas, Charles, *Tintagel Castle* (English Heritage).

Wallington, Mark, *500 Mile Walkies* (Hutchinson/Arrow, 1986).

Wilkinson, Gerald, *Woodland Walks in South West England* (OS and Webb & Bower, 1986).

Ordnance Survey Maps covering the South West Coast Path (Minehead to Padstow)

Landranger Maps: 180, 181, 190, 200.

Outdoor Leisure Map: 9 Exmoor.

Explorer Map: 106 Newquay & Padstow, 109 Bodmin Moor, 111 Bude, Boscastle & Tintagel, 126 Clovelly & Hartland, 139 Bideford, Ilfracombe & Barnstaple.

Motoring Maps: Reach the South West Coast Path by car using Travelmaster Map 8, 'South West England and South Wales'.